WE NOW BELONG
TO OURSELVES

WE NOW BELONG
TO OURSELVES

WE NOW BELONG TO OURSELVES

J. L. EDMONDS, THE BLACK PRESS, AND BLACK CITIZENSHIP IN AMERICA

ARIANNE EDMONDS

OXFORD
UNIVERSITY PRESS

OXFORD
UNIVERSITY PRESS

Oxford University Press is a department of the University of Oxford.
It furthers the University's objective of excellence in research, scholarship,
and education by publishing worldwide. Oxford is a registered trade mark of
Oxford University Press in the UK and in certain other countries.

Published in the United States of America by Oxford University Press
198 Madison Avenue, New York, NY 10016, United States of America.

CIP data is on file at the Library of Congress

ISBN 9780197579084

DOI: 10.1093/oso/9780197579084.001.0001

Printed by Integrated Books International, United States of America

The manufacturer's authorised representative in the EU for product safety is Oxford University Press España S.A. of El Parque Empresarial
San Fernando de Henares, Avenida de Castilla, 2 – 28830 Madrid (www.oup.es/en or product.safety@oup.com). OUP España S.A. also acts as
importer into Spain of products made by the manufacturer.

FSC
MIX
Paper
FSC® C183721

For Jefferson

Dedicated to my beloved mom and dad, my sweet husband JoeJoe,
and our angel baby Adina

Contents

A Love Note to Readers

When you read this book and let the words and the stories wash over you, know that it is both me and my beloved Jefferson speaking to you. Together, both earthbound and in spirit form, we come to you humbly to share what we know and love about Black people in America and in the diaspora. We'll tell you of the places we've traveled to get closer to ourselves and closer to a sense of home and comfort. Together, we'll analyze our experiences and tell you stories of the people we loved and the people who didn't know how to love us back. We'll share places we needed to seek refuge and the places that provided us a cool breeze, a place to rest, and a place of sanctuary. While I've spent the last decade collecting stories within my own family and studying Black Angeleno migration patterns, it was my dear Jefferson who lived it. It was he who had the foresight to collect, document, and share these stories with his community. He spoke of me, my dad, and our descendants when he wrote about why he did this work. I will do the same with all of you. This story is a collection of fragmented histories quilted together with both my own and my great-great-grandfather's hands. Together, we'll show the city of Los Angeles, the place we made our home. The place we put down roots and the place that helped us redefine family.

Prologue: Seeds from the Ancestors

In my grandma's middle room, there are six long wooden shelves that house my great-great-grandfather Jefferson's personal library. You'll find *Arabian Nights*, the *Iliad and Odyssey* by Homer, and the original printing of the *Souls of Black Folks* by W. E. B. Du Bois. I've passed these books thousands of times. My cousins Naqeeb, Khalid, and I would reenact *Xena: Warrior Princess* fighting scenes using old Christmas paper rolls as swords and cut-out paper plates as her infamous Chakram. I was of course Xena; my only-child Leo moon wouldn't let me play a supporting character—ever. There's a dusty old domino set sitting on the top shelf, a ceramic pair of bears playing on a seesaw, and my grandma's stuffed Dobermann dog sitting watch over the books in our family library.

We bumped up against those bookshelves hundreds of times and placed our cranberry apple Juicy Juice boxes on the shelves over the years. Along the side of the wall near the bookshelves, my dad would measure our height every year and mark our initials. Today, after thirty-five years, the etched record of our yearly sprouting is still documented in blue and black ink. The casual nature of these books was certainly a statement about the legacy of our family. It was just there. It was important enough to keep and preserve and be respected, but it wasn't revered. Nor would these books ever be added to the yard sales my grandma and my Aunt Marla would host every summer on the front lawn. They were just part of the fabric of the house, like the mid-century modern light fixtures in the front room or my grandpa's Don Ho cassette tapes collecting dust in the back guest room. It all just sat there, not to be engaged but not to be discarded. It sat there waiting. Waiting for me. Waiting to be explored. Waiting to be loved on. I pulled out the match, but my dad set the fire. He taught me how to care for our archive, the value of it. He showed me how and when we'd start sharing the brilliant mind, life, and legacy of Jefferson Lewis Edmonds.

I went looking for my great-great-grandfather, Jefferson Lewis Edmonds, in 2009. I did it because I wanted to be closer to my dad. My parents split when I was pretty young. By the time I was thirteen my mom and I had moved to Atlanta, just over 2,000 miles away from the City of Angels and the place my family had made their home since the 1880s. Researching and piecing together our family history became something that helped close the gap from the years and miles between my dad and me. When we couldn't talk about all the life that was missed by being apart for so long, we would fill the air with stories of Jefferson and his newspaper, *The Liberator*—and how we'd make sure his legacy in Los Angeles would be remembered. Jefferson helped us find our way back to one another.

My father's side of the family always emphasized the importance of education, investing in local politics, and sticking to traditions. These were values I had to grow into. Becoming a mother helped me understand that those values and structures were all powerful forms of love and stability, and long-lasting acts of service. I didn't know that digging into my great-great-grandfather's library, reading his notes, and spending time with our family newspaper would help illuminate where those core values came from. I went looking because I was curious and wanted to feel a connection to my dad. What I found was that the seed Jefferson planted for us almost 140 years ago was still taking root and still blooming in me, my dad, and my whole family.

*

So many Black families in the United States can only trace their history back to their grandparents. The erasure of our stories and records is devastating. We have movements like Black Lives Matter that help address the brutality and violence against our bodies and psyche. We've had movements like the civil rights era in the 1960s, that attempted to address inequality and demand policy changes and national political power. Currently we see a revolution around Black rest, like the powerful work of the Nap ministry led by Nap Bishop Tricia Hersey, reminding Black people in America to exit the hustle culture train and focus on mental health and personal dreams. The last frontier that our Black social movements have not been able to address is how we should restore our history, our memories, and our family lore. What becomes of them? So many of our stories start and end with enslavement. Unknowingly I set out to change that narrative and help unearth Jefferson's legacy and that of so many Black Angeleno families in the process. I've been doing restoration work. I've been making room for all the stories that were thrown to the bottom of the ocean, made to drown. Bit by bit I've been bringing them to the shore, drying them off, and sharing with those around me the great tale of my great-great-grandfather, Jefferson Lewis Edmonds.

Since the start of this project I've felt a responsibility to make *The Liberator* public and make it accessible. Our partnership with the Los Angeles Public Library made that hope a reality. Through funding from the California State Library system, our family newspaper was digitized and archived online not only for researchers and scholars, but as a resource for Black people to find their family, like I did. I wanted their world to change and have meaning by rooting them in their own legacies. My work reaches underneath the family tree, beyond Black family values, and attempts to examine our relationship with the United States. Jefferson used his voice to help shape Black citizenship and, in this generation, I'm seeking to understand if the roots of all his efforts still hold today.

Citizenship is a direct link to lineage, and the Black press served as an attempt to create a record and an account of our existence. Citizenship is belonging. That is what Jefferson was fighting for. Much like the Black Lives Matter mantra "Say Their Names," I have helped to unlock these archives so the world wouldn't forget what we've done, where we've been, and all the places we are headed! So I went searching in public libraries, universities, archives, digital records, and filing cabinets at my grandma's house. I met with historians, archivists, and librarians from institutions all over the country. I thought I was looking for Jefferson, but what I found instead was me. I found reflections of a time over a century ago that closely mirror the world in which I live today—all the turmoil, destruction, and social upheaval of a country grappling with historical and cultural amnesia. Jefferson fought the same beasts. I didn't know it, but I went looking for his blueprint.

If Jefferson could set a vision for our family that can still be accessed in the present day, almost a century and a half later, then what other intentions, visions, prayers, and hopes were passed down for us? My research for this book took me past the 400 years of American slavery, past the transatlantic trade and onto the shores of the Atlantic in West Africa. What did they wish for us? What promise did they make to us?

PART I

What We Brought with Us

The Stories That We Carry

The waves from the Atlantic Ocean crashed loudly and violently along the coast every time I made the voyage to the Elmina Castle slave dungeons off the coast of Ghana. These waves would wail and ache as they splashed along the steps leading to the Door of No Return, the same door used to transport millions of African people to places unknown. It was as if those waves carried all the warnings and last requests back to the family that for so long had gone unanswered. After each tour, I'd sit on one of the rocks along the coast and listen to her majesty—the sea, Mami Wata, Yemanjá, our water goddess, our mother—and ask her what she wanted me to tell my family back home. I'd asked her what she wanted me to tell all of you. All I heard was, "Don't forget us."

"Where do I go from here?" I'd ask myself.

Perhaps we need to dive into what got us here.

*

Millions of African people would be brought to Cape Coast, marched through the countryside to their last bath at the river in Assin Manso before reaching Elmina Castle. All from different tribes, all with different tongues, all with different ways of being. Cramped together waiting, waiting, waiting in the dark. Waiting for a sign, hearing the ocean and yet still waiting.

Women would be held in the dungeons closest to the door of no return, closest to the ocean, closest to the way out. Together they waited with their children, separated from their men, and sequestered in dungeons at the center of the castle. They waited weeks, sometimes months, for ships to come. Listening to the waves crashing against the only wall separating them and the vast Atlantic.

According to the research of Judith Carney and Richard Nicholas Rosomoff, "Africa's botanical legacy traveled with its peoples and improved the sustenance of millions across a vast intercontinental trading network. The African diaspora was one of plants and peoples" (Carney and Rosomoff 2011, 124). While the European captors saw the provisions these enslaved Africans brought on board as a critical component to keeping them alive, Black American ancestors saw the provisions as an opportunity to stay connected to their homes, their culture, and their humanity. They stored the black-eyed peas, yams, and okra seeds during the voyage and planted them as soon as they reached the new world (Grimé 1976).

Today, these items are staples in Black American homes and speak to the intentions and foresight of generations past. This act of survival and legacy illustrates a dynamic system of communal decision-making that was first birthed in Africa, traveled to the Americas, and became the foundation for how we care for one another. Perhaps the hiding and planting shows us that our enslaved ancestors were always two steps ahead and always thinking about how to plant, sow, and harvest little reminders and signs that they were always thinking of us. They've always been praying for us and preparing for us.

*

We were heading to the Melcom Super Mall on Spintex Road on a Sunday in August in 2022. While sitting in traffic near the roundabout at Palace Mall, my husband turned on the radio. He's our resident DJ in the car, so I was surprised he let the radio take the lead this time. A very catchy dance remix started playing, but it was the words that caught my attention. I remember closing my eyes and hearing a sorrowful woman's voice singing in Ga. The song was so upbeat, playful almost. But her voice was haunting. As the song went on I held my heart, and my breathing became labored. My husband turned to me and asked if I was okay. I burst into tears. I said to him, "What is she saying? Why is my heart aching like this?"

He didn't take his eye off the road but he grabbed my hand. He said:

This song is about you. It's an old, old, old song that we sing during the Homowo festival. It's about remembering what happened to us. What happened to our family. Remembering who we've lost.

He then began translating for me as tears continued to roll down my face:

> *Our ancestor*
> *Our ancestor*
> *You have to wake up*
> *Your people are suffering*
> *Did you sell us?*
> *Before you died?*
> *Did any country colonize us*
> *Before you died?*
> *What did you discuss with the whites?*
> *And today they have sold us?*

A major focal point of the Homowo festival is family, connection, and celebration of the harvest. It's about paying homage to the times when the Ga people experienced famine and how important it is to celebrate and show gratitude for a fruitful and bountiful new beginning. For us, the taken ones, to be included, thought of, celebrated, and prayed for after all these hundreds of years is something I'm still sitting with. To this day, the memory of this song brings me to tears. Gratitude is what continues to bubble up for me.

For all the times I was convinced that we were the forgotten ones, floating and unrooted— hearing that song helped me reframe how I see myself, my family, and our future. No longer are we the taken ones whose spirits hover over the Atlantic Ocean while our feet stand firmly planted in the Americas.

Our souls' journey back to the continent is not an easy one. The reunion is bittersweet. We don't fully belong on the continent or the

Americas and Caribbean. So much time, so much pain and neglect has torn us apart. Hearing that song was a start. A start of a new beginning, a reminder that a new story can emerge at any point. A story that I'll hand down to my children and their children. I'll tell them we carried these stories for you. We've been preparing for you. We've been praying for you.

That song reminded me of the prayers, the hopes, and the dreams Jefferson had for us with his newspaper, *The Liberator*. He welcomed all those willing to travel and start something new. He promised them that he would help create a new world where they could find belonging. A place where someone was waiting for them. A place where someone was preparing for them.

Jefferson

My Beloved Jefferson,

It was you who taught me how to speak up. You showed me how to reach toward the heavens and pull down the type of life I wanted to live. You showed me that we can pierce into the fabric of our American democracy and slowly, carefully dissect and reassemble a type of liberation that we deserve. A liberation that we've already fought for. You invited me into your vision when you left us your library, your notes, and all your newspapers. Those papers passed through so many hands. For a century your words were kept, protected by the Carlisle family, the Osbornes, my grandma, my grandpa, my dad, and now me. Before Los Angeles celebrated you in this century, your work was whispered only among academic circles and historians. Thank you for letting me share your story with all of us. It's been one of the great honors of my life.

CHAPTER I

Finding Jefferson

We first find my great-great-grandfather, Jefferson Lewis Edmonds, in Crawford, Mississippi, in the 1850s. He, like his grandson Walter Chase Edmonds Jr. and my dad, kept a record of his life, his passions, and his daily activities. I'm assuming Jefferson wanted someone to find him and the life he led. Well, I did, and I made it one of my missions to share the stories he left behind. You'll see me referring to my beloved Jefferson through this book. Using his first name helps me humanize him and make him feel more like family, and not just a distant historical figure.

Jefferson was born in Lowsdale County, Mississippi, on the Edmonds plantation in 1852. According to census records I was able to collect over the years (with the help of my dear cousin Dawson), Jefferson shared with his census numerator that he was born in October 1852. It's hard to say how accurate that information is, for so many slave records only list a year, and very few offer exact dates. If he was in fact born in October, Jefferson's appreciation for beautiful design and a community of cooperation and mutual support rings true of his Libra legacy.

Before Jefferson moved his family to Los Angeles for a fresh start, he would first learn to read and write through the Freedmen's Bureau schools that were established during the Reconstruction era in the mid-1860s. By 1875, Jefferson began teaching grade school and canvassing for voter rights for Black men in the state of Mississippi. He worked tirelessly to get Black legislators elected and sent to Washington. According to a December 18, 1914, *California Eagle* retrospective, Jefferson was elected justice of the peace (twice) and served in the lower house of the state legislature in Mississippi in the 1880s. This first half of his life would be the training ground for *The Liberator*, the powerful Black newspaper he would become most known for.

After several death threats and the constant resistance to civic change by white Southerners, Jefferson was forced to change course. He would be confronted with the fact that his efforts could only take him so far. Mississippi wasn't quite ready for true civic change and fully realized Black American citizenship. Jefferson was seeking liberation, but at the core he wanted his people to have a place to belong. He desired a place of ease and fertile ground to start something bold and new.

At the turn of the twentieth century, Jefferson took a leap of faith and moved westward. He first stepped in as editor of the *Pasadena Search-light* newspaper (as will be discussed later in the book). This was followed by his more notable achievement as an editor of *The Liberator* newspaper. While many formerly enslaved Black Americans moved to the East Coast and Midwest during the Reconstruction era, many stayed in the South and began working in sharecropping schemes under their former plantation owners. Jefferson sought to interrupt that reality, aiming to shift the narrative and establish a new route with his reporting in *The Liberator*.

In efforts to lure Black Southerners to make the trek out west, Jefferson ran ads to promote ticket sales for the Santa Fe Railroad Line heading to Southern California with stops in Memphis and New Orleans. He incorporated a "City by the Sea" announcements section to showcase the elevated new Black American lifestyle out west: "The Don't Worry Club of Santa Monica entertained the visitors by the sea at the home of Miss Brown on South Main street, Tuesday evening the 29th," *The Liberator* declared on September 1, 1911. Jefferson knew that life could be so much more, but leaving the South would be the first step. He printed in a September 1901 issue of *The Liberator* that "the only thing that we are proud of in connection with the fact that we were born in the South is that we left it." Jefferson knew that in order to expand and build

something for himself and his family he would have to leave everything
he knew.

*

Jefferson arrived in California in the early 1890s and would continue
the work of an already thriving, civically engaged free Black community.
Delilah Beasley's book *The Negro Trail Blazers* shares that there were free
Black men and women living in California during Spanish rule, prior
to the state joining the Union in 1850. Many of them arrived on trading ships and earned money to pay for their freedom. They purchased
homes and built businesses. The passing of the Compromise of 1850
stipulated that California be a slavery free state. However, the amended
Fugitive Slave Act, enacted the same year, mandated that any enslaved
person found in any free state would be returned to their enslaver. These
laws didn't stop enterprising white Southern slave owners from traveling
out west for gold and new opportunities. Often they would force groups
of enslaved people from their plantations to join their caravans (Beasley
1919).

Black communities all across the state of California went to great
lengths to alert the newcomers that they had legal protections. A
notable example would be Bridget "Biddy" Mason. Mason arrived in
San Bernardino, California, in 1851 with her enslaver, Robert Smith,
along with her daughters and a caravan of enslaved men and women.
Smith set out to establish Mormon settlements in the American West
and refused to heed warnings of California's free state laws. Upon their
arrival, Mason began connecting with the free Black community in Los
Angeles. By 1856, the community helped her raise funds to secure legal
counsel to sue Smith for her freedom. She won her court case and went
on to become a prominent businesswoman, philanthropist, and midwife
in Los Angeles (Reiniche 2023).

A more infamous freedom case took place in 1858, in the San Francisco area. Lee, an enslaved man from Mississippi, was brought to Sacra-
mento by his enslaver, Charles Stovall. Lee was hired out to perform

various duties to help fund Stovall's ventures. Much like the Biddy Mason case, the small but mighty Black community mobilized on his behalf, working tirelessly to secure funding for his legal battles and to provide the support he needed to secure his freedom (Beasley 1919).

Jefferson would join a group of Black Californians who were fighting for legal protections nearly a century before the civil rights movement erupted in the 1950s and 1960s. Their work laid the foundation for political advancement at the turn of the twentieth century. Jefferson continued the work of these trailblazing civil advocates and created pathways for those willing to leave the South for a new life.

*

The Black press before and after emancipation played a critical role in shaping and transforming intellectual and civic life for Black Americans. One could argue that owning and operating a Black newspaper publication at the turn of the century would be at the same scale as owning a TV network or large-scale film production company today. It was a major feat to build your own platform, organize ad sales, foster engaged readership, and keep consistent subscriptions year after year.

Jefferson stood among some of the greats in the Black press at the turn of the century. Dr. Lonnie Bunch III, scholar and founding director of the National Museum of African American History and Culture, wrote, "As a leader and a visionary in the struggle against racism in Southern California, Edmonds deserves the scholarly attention and reputation garnered by his contemporaries William Monroe Trotter, editor of the *Boston Guardian*, and Robert Abbott, publisher of the *Chicago Defender*" (Bunch 2001, 131). According to Jefferson, *The Liberator* had close to 3,000 subscriptions toward the end of the newspaper's run, with both local and national subscribers. This would mean that nearly half of Black Angelenos in Los Angeles subscribed to the newspaper at the time, making *The Liberator* an anchor for the emerging Black Angeleno citizens.

Jefferson would go on to create a powerful network of educated, civic-minded community conscious Black Angelenos hailing from all over the

South. Through *The Liberator* he would encourage Black Americans to come to Los Angeles for a fresh start and provide instruction on new life as Black American citizens. However, his fight for liberation came with battle wounds and isolation.

While admired by his peers for his commitment to advancing Black citizenship and civic engagement, he still was quite contrarian in some of his views. The *California Eagle* newspaper said this of Jefferson's passing in January 1914:

> We believe that the highest compliment we can pay ourselves is to mention the ex-slave who, untutored, rose to be a "force in his realm." Therefore, while we did not agree with J. L. Edmonds in hardly anything, we differed as humans and not as beasts. Hence our relations were always friendly and each in our own way fought as we thought best in, our own way for the uplift of a race.

Jefferson spoke out against injustices against the Black Angeleno community. He railed against unfair housing, discriminatory legislation, and inadequate educational opportunities for Black students. But he also directed his gaze inward to call out Black Angelenos who didn't support his political views. Many times he'd cross party lines if a viable candidate proved they would fight for the Black community. This divisive behavior caused tension and created distance from some of his freedom fighter peers. Editor-in-chief Joseph Blackburn Bass of the *California Eagle* recounted in a November 24, 1933, edition of the paper that he grew fond of Jefferson in the few years he knew him before his passing: "Each issue was looked forward to because the populace wanted to know who next would be on the griddle in the columns of *The Liberator* . . . they loved him for the enemies he made." Bass shared his sense of relief that he managed to avoid being "attacked" in the pages of *The Liberator*.

Perhaps Jefferson's zealous approach was because he knew what was at stake. He was enslaved in his lifetime, and he worked tirelessly to ensure that future generations would not have to experience that same bondage. He had a mandate to tell the truth and not leave anything out. He refused to be silenced. His humanity, his struggles, and his triumphs truly shine when you look at the full breadth of his literal journey. His paper reported on all the ways Black Angelenos should come together and fight for their rights. The pages of *The Liberator* championed women's rights, equitable education for Black students, and homeownership. Jefferson yearned for a sense of belonging, connection, and a community he could fight alongside. But his forward-thinking political views were not always mainstream, and this would create division and challenges for him toward the end of his life. Later in the book I'll delve into some of the roadblocks he faced being such an outspoken leader and political commentator.

Yet Jefferson dared to dream big. He dared to create a powerful new world for Black Angelenos who may not have understood his uncharted path. Time and history showed that many of the initiatives, policies, and elections Jefferson championed would swing toward progress for the Black Angeleno. Nearly thirty years after Jefferson's death, the *California Eagle* shared this in a section of the paper titled "California's Great Journalistic Pioneers": "Edmonds's fiery 'Liberator' was a trailblazer among West Coast Negro journals" (1941). The San Francisco–based Black newspaper *Western Outlook* added on January 4th, 1914, that "he was an able thinker and was a close reasoner. His editorials, though often keen and biting, always commanded attention" (Beasley 1919, 260). Jefferson was admired and respected for his fierce loyalty to the Black community and his command over words, but the records show that many feared his wrath and the sharp point of his pen.

Man Emancipated

In 1909, Jefferson was commissioned to write an article (and likely asked to support the editorial process) of an eight-page special edition spread for the *Los Angeles Daily Times* to honor Abraham Lincoln's 100th birthday. At this point, Jefferson was already a notable newspaper editor, farmer, real estate entrepreneur, father, and husband. He was close to the end of his life at this point. The piece ran on February 12, 1909, and it was part retrospective, part future-casting that showcased how Black Americans were advancing forty years after enslavement (Edmonds 1909). He joined fellow Black leaders across the country to discuss the starting of businesses, the purchasing of homes, and the Black cities being built in Los Angeles and its surrounding areas. Booker T. Washington was invited to write about the national Black perspective. Together they painted a picture of Los Angeles as a city that was innovative, prosperous, and on the precipice of a Black renaissance.

We'll explore later how that dream was challenged at almost every turn. But let's first hear from my dear Jefferson's own story of liberation:

HOW FREEDOM'S WORD FOUND THE BONDMAN
by J. L. Edmonds of Sawtelle, A Former Slave

When in 1619 that old Dutch kidnapper sold twenty negroes as slaves to the Virginians, only a god could have foreseen the tremendous, far-reaching results that that little transaction was to produce. It was, perhaps, God's way to bring two heterogeneous peoples into sympathetic touch for the civilization and development of two dark continents. The Christianization

Figure 1.1 Jefferson Lewis Edmonds, "How Freedom's Word Found the Boundman," featured on the cover of the *Los Angeles Daily Times*, February 12, 1909. Lincoln Financial Foundation Collection. https://archive.org /details/losangelesdaily1219mark/page/n27/mode/2up

of negro savages captured in the jungles of Africa and their elevation to the priceless boon of American citizenship, is the greatest missionary achievement in the annals of the last half-dozen centuries. And yet, the parties engaged in the scheme were actuated by the most sordid motives that ever degraded the human soul. As I follow the negro's struggle upward from barbarism through enslavement to civilization, and witness the return of negro missionaries with their lamps all trimmed and burning with the fire of Christian enlightenment, to light up the dark places of their ancestral home, I cannot but exclaim:

"God moves in a mysterious way,
His wonders to perform."

What effect has the negro's presence in this country had upon its history? Let's see: If we erase from American history the pages that the negro's presence caused to be written, it would be a short, uninteresting story. Remove from the American political stage the illustrious actors placed there by the negro's presence, and the curtain would fall upon the departure of George Washington, Thomas Jefferson, and Benjamin Franklin. If the negroes had not visited this country as slaves the battles of our great Civil War would never have been fought. The unflinching courage displayed by the blue and the gray, in their charge and counter-charge on Cemetery Hill, the battle above the clouds and the bloody struggle of the Wilderness would not "go sounding down the ages." As proof of American civil and military genius, Lincoln, John Brown, Garrison, Phillips, Sumner, Mrs. Harriet Beecher Stowe and Lovejoy and Grant, and Lee, and their illustrious lieutenants, would have taken their

"Chambers in the silent halls of death,"
And our own Frederick Douglass would not have been.

Mr. Lincoln regarded the presence of the negro soldiers in the Union army as being so indispensable, that he said: "If the 150,000 negro soldiers now in the army were taken therefrom and placed in the Confederate army or in the Confederate cornfield, the cause of the Union would not survive six weeks." But I must hurry along to Freedom's day.

One day, Nelse, the errand boy, said "Jeff," speaking to me, "do you know we is gwine to be free?"

"What is that?" I asked.

"We'll be like master's children; have nothing to do but play and go to school, and go where you please. Mr. Lincum, a big man up in the norf is gwine to make us free."

Nothing more was said, but I began to do what I had never done before— to think. Throwing aside the things that had before engaged my childish mind, I gave myself up to thinking of freedom, of being like "master's children," of going to school and going where I pleased. How all this was to be brought about next engaged my thoughts. After going over the whole matter, I concluded that there was no man or men big enough to break the master's power, and make me free as his children. However, Nelse had created a new world for me; I now saw things as I had never seen them before, and was seized with "A nameless longing

For something better than I had known."

Finally, night brought my mother home from the field and, looking thoughtfully into the blazing fire while she was preparing the evening meal, which consisted of cornpone and bacon, I said, "Mamma, Nelse says, Mr. Lincum is gwine to make us free; is it true?"

With a look of horror and surprise she seized me and gave me a violent shake, saying as she did so: "You had better never say that again. If the white folks hear that they'll hang you and Nelse both."

This violent turn of affairs frightened me severely and spoiled my usually good appetite. From my mother's actions I was convinced that there was something in the wind. Thenceforward I was a changed boy, for, with the knowledge of freedom and its opportunities, came also the full meaning of slavery. Though I had awakened to my undone condition, the belief that I would someday be free made life as free from care as before. For what a panacea for present ills is a steadfast, absorbing belief in the coming of a brighter day.

Nelse's duty as errand boy was to carry supplies from the plantation to Master's residence in Crawford, an aristocratic village ten miles distant, and to take messages from place to place and do odd jobs. The position was a very desirable one and meant not only a trip or more to town each week, with many side trips thrown in, but the holder was the recipient of many presents at the big house for faithful performance of duties. The errand boy was regarded as a person of distinction: being half free, his word was authority. His frequent visits to town made him a sort of purchasing agent for the slaves who bestowed upon him their sincere blessings. Nelse was a big-hearted, intelligent boy, possibly 16, who had a kind word for every person he met.

The next good tidings he brought me was the information that I was to take his place as errand boy. After giving me the necessary introductions about the duties of my new position he took charge of a plow team and became the plow manager's favorite. As an errand boy, I received my first lessons in personal responsibility. With a one-horse wagonload of supplies I made my first trip to Crawford. If, with your mind's eye, you take a peep at the long rows of one and two-room log cabins occupied by Master's slaves, the largest and most commodious dwellings I had ever seen, you can imagine my feelings as I stood on the main street of that cultured village with its wilderness of splendid, attractive residences, two to three stories high and as white as snow. And for my life I could not figure out why so many people thronged the streets in their Sunday clothes. When I started to town, the woman who was in charge of the dairy and whose duty it was to prepare butter, eggs, and poultry for the big house, said: "Take care of Buckra," meaning the overseer's boy, who was accompanying me to town to show me the way. With a knowing look she said: "A still tongue makes a wise head. It won't do to talk about all you see and hear."

On my return, the entire Black population of little folks turned out to hear the news. It was then that I discovered that the admonition given me by the good dairy woman was unnecessary. I had seen wonders, but for want of words my tongue was still. I couldn't tell anything. I was face to face with a kind of poverty that is hard to describe. Although the white boy had made several trips to town I found him to be as poverty-stricken in the matter of words as I was. Among themselves the slaves always referred to the overseer and members of their families as "buckra," denoting contempt. As errand boy I lived in a new atmosphere. I saw slavery and much of the country as I had not seen them before. In going from farm to farm in the performance of my duties, I soon realized that "slavery was the sum of all villainies," a curse with few, if any, mitigations. I saw many of the scenes described in Uncle Tom's Cabin enacted in real life. But in the dust of oblivion lies the slave and his unfortunate tormentor: here let them rest.

A GREAT SLAVE PLANTATION

Dr. J. L. Edmonds, my master, was kind and indulgent to his slaves. He and his wife were Virginians of noble blood. My mother and grandmother and all of the older slaves were also Virginians from near Culpeper Courthouse that had been handed down from father to son for so many generations that the ties of friendship between them were more like those of family than of master and slave. Kindness and culture were traits of the Edmonds family that radiated from master to slave, from the great house to the plantation, blessing all with whom they came in contact.

The system in vogue in the management of the plantation was perfect, the labor being divided into several departments each under separate foremen. The hoe hands were made up of old men, boys, women and children. Then there were the plow hands and the departments of carpentry and blacksmithing. One man with assistants looked after the horses and cattle. A man and wife and assistants had charge of dairying, poultrying, and fruit drying. Each foreman was responsible for the management of his department. The overseer was a . . . of general superintendent and . . . of difficulties—sometimes creating them—and to give passes to slaves desiring to visit distant friends and relatives. These foremen, besides conferring with the overseer in all matters relative to their departments, made full and complete reports to master on his periodical visits to the plantation. The central idea of the system was to increase individual efficiency and at the same time reduce the possibility of friction to a minimum. It was a system based upon personal integrity and worked so well that, if the law had not required the presence of a white man on each plantation occupied by slaves, master would have dispensed with the overseer altogether.

The space occupied by the slave quarters covered more than a half section, each family was given an allotment of land for truck gardening, the amount depending on the size of the family. Each cabin was fenced to itself surrounded by fruit and ornamental trees as individual tastes suggested.

Many of the slaves added to their allotments by clearing wood land. By working at night by moonlight or torch light and on their weekly half holidays the slaves produced thousands of dollars' worth of cotton, tobacco and potatoes annually which found a ready market at good prices. As a means of encouragement, the master would buy most of their products, paying cash. And strange as it may seem, he owned several wealthy slaves who purchased forty-acre farms in 1887, paying for it in gold and silver.

RELIGION AMONG THE SLAVES

The slaves were by nature religious and master encouraged this sentiment among them in every way possible. He had a church erected in the center of their quarters and hired a white minister to preach to them twice a month. Local negro preachers were ordained who conducted religious services in his absence. This produced a high standard of morality among them. The slaves composed their own songs, some of them the most soul-stirring I ever heard, every song a plea to God for deliverance from slavery. How often have I heard those plaintive notes by which the slaves laid their grievances at the throne of God. In spite of master's solicitude for the welfare of his slaves, they were often victims of outrageous treatment by brutal overseers. Then, too, it is impossible to treat a slave kind enough to make him love slavery better than freedom. Kind treatment increases one's intelligence and intelligence and slavery cannot dwell happily together in the same soul.

DANCING, TOO

While the religious sentiment of the slaves was diligently cultivated, singing, dancing and innocent sports were also encouraged. A good dancer was about as popular as a good preacher. While I have the utmost confidence in the sincerity and genuineness of the religion of the master's family, I must confess that although I never saw them at a plantation prayer meeting they often dignified the plantation dance by their presence. I understand it now. Fifty slave men and women engaged in a cotillion presented a scene of animation that baffles description. Seated on a raised platform with his head nodding to every movement of his bow, the fiddler was the motive power for the whole entrancing scene, with every fiber of his body in motion, and the dancers going through their graceful rapid evolutions, he would break in:

> *"Shoo my honey, shoo my love,*
> *"Shoo my pretty little turtle dove."*

Again after a short interval:

> *"Let it rain, let it snow,*
> *My little wife's in Baltimore."*

Standing by him next in power is the stalwart fellow who calls the figures, with his body swaying from side to side like a bush in a gale, he is generator of animation.

Sometimes, even now, I see in my imagination the pine torch lighting up the old dance cabin, long since fallen to decay: the fiddler, the dancers and the spectators and everything as I knew it in the days of yore.

THE WAR BREAKS OUT

The beating of drums, the tramping of steeds, the tread of marching feet broke the monotony of slave life, and proclaimed the news that the call to war had been sounded. They expected it. They had heard of the Lincoln-Douglass debates, and the Sumner-Brooks encounter. Then the daily passing of long files of men in martial array told them that the day of deliverance from slavery was at hand. It was the breaking of the day after their long night of bondage; they had at last reached the shores of slavery's Red Sea. If the overseer did not discover a change in the demeanor of the slaves, I cannot see why. The plaintive note in their songs changed to one of joy; the prophecy of freedom beyond the grave that had previously been the burden of their songs, now told of freedom here below. Thus:

> *"After the day of jubilee,*
> *There'll be no more cuttin' and slashin'."*

This and many similar rude stanzas were sung both day and night. Everybody was light-hearted and gay as they went on performing their daily tasks.

Accompanied by his two sons, Nevel and Jefferson, "Old Masters" came to see them bid farewell to the slaves before leaving for the war. At the noon hour all of the slaves were summoned to the overseer's house. Master made a speech, telling us that war had broken out, that times were going to be hard, but said it would all be over in ninety days, and expressed his confidence in each of us doing our duty on the farm as his two noble sons would do on the field'. And we did, without a single exception. It was a pathetic scene—nearly a thousand people in tears. The two young men, splendid pictures of nobility, looking so grand and gay in their faultless uniforms, stood for quite a while in the embrace of two Black women—their nurses. Aunt Dolly, with her face bathed in tears, embraced Master Nevel, and my mother embraced Master Jefferson. The leave-taking of those two black women was as affectionate as it could possibly be.

The news of great battles soon began to pour in, and white men grew scarcer and scarcer, until not a man able to bear arms was left. My father, who was manager of the hoe hands, was put in charge of the plantation. The slaves were kept well informed as to the progress of the war. Their sources of information were the house servants, several of whom could read and write. The poor white women who depended upon the slaves to keep them from starving while their husbands were at the front, and a wealthy Union man named Harvey, who refused to fight against the Union, killed a Confederate conscripting officer and took refuge on our farm and in adjacent swamps till the war closed.

THE GREAT NEWS COMES

It was a lovely day in May, 1865. The forest surrounding our plantation on every side was arrayed in its spring dress and nature wore a smile such as she wears only in our sea-girt Southland. The public road, fenced in, ran east and west through our farm. The hoe hands, several hundred in number, were hoeing corn near the road. While singing merrily a horseman was seen hurrying westward down the lane. The rider, as black as the charger on which he rode, proved to be the coachman, my grandmother's brother. There was something unusual about his movements. We had seen him come along that road several times before riding slowly, the bearer of sad tidings—some member of master's family had passed away and he came to summon everybody to the funeral. On one occasion, with tear-wet face, he summoned us to the funeral of Master Nevel, who had been killed at Antietam; next he summoned us to old master's funeral—the hardest blow of all. He had died of a broken heart, caused by the death of a noble son.

But on this occasion, hat in hand, his black charger, white with foam, on he came. Everybody stopped. A breathless silence prevailed. Halting his horse in front of the people, he waved his hat above his head, exclaiming at the top of his voice:

"Everybody is free! Everybody is free!"

This was the signal for one of the most thrilling scenes I have ever witnessed. In an instant every hoe was dropped, the people being seized with a wild frenzy. Some wept aloud for joy. Men and women embraced each other. Others rolled over and over in the dust. Staid old men, screaming as if mad, ran hither and thither. While this wild medley of capers were being enacted, some one yelled:

"Go and tell the plow hands!"

TORE DOWN THE FENCE

In less time than it takes to write it a dozen willing hands tore down the fence, and the foaming horse that had been rearing upon its hind feet and prancing as if he, too, was enjoying the scene, dashed headlong with his rider to the plow gang a half mile distant. Hearing the noise made by the hoe hands, every plow man had stopped. Rushing madly among them, Uncle Henry in a dramatic way told the news. As if by magic, every horse was unharnessed and mounted. And, like a troop of cavalry, with yells and amid clouds of dust, many of them bareheaded, they dashed among the hoe hands. They rode round and round, up and down the lane. Some exclaiming as they rode: "I am free! I am free, and I don't care who

knows it!" Nelse was shouting: "I told you so! I told you so!" Now Uncle
Henry made a dash for the quarters to carry the news to the old and decrepit
and such as were confined to their homes by sickness or misfortune, the
mixed army of horsemen and pedestrians following him. On reaching the
quarters, the wild scenes were reenacted. The sick, the lame and the halt
joined in the festivities, and for the time being the old were young again,
the lame could run and the sick were well. Women, weeping, seized their
children, pressed them to their bosoms, saying: "You is mine! You is mine!
There'll be no more sellin' and buyin'."

Yelling like mad, the plow men rode all over the quarters, yelling
freedom at every cabin door.

BACK TO WORK

It was a great day. The prayers of many generations had been answered.
Standing still, performing their duties well, they had seen the salvation
of God. After two days spent in thanksgiving and prayer and fiddling
and dancing, my father called together the head men and it was decided
that everybody should return to work. At the blowing of the horn on the
third day, work was resumed as usual, only a few young men being absent,
who returned some days later. Several days or weeks later, Master James
came over and announced that all who signed a contract and remained
would receive a part of the crops as wages, stating that all were as free as
he. He read the contract, and every man, woman and child who worked
was requested to come up and make his or her mark. The people, both old
and young, responded promptly. When it came my time I swung back,
thinking that I might be signing away my freedom. While I had received
the news of it in silence and sadness as I thought of future separations
from early friends and scenes that freedom must entail, I was not willing
to sign it away. After considerable persuasion, I finally made my mark.
Thinking in after years how it must have humiliated Master James, it
has been to me a source of sincere regret. In the early '70s when I was
struggling for the rudiments of an education, in order to assist me he

made me special deputy and bailiff in his court. He, his brother Jefferson, and Mrs. Turner, their sister, were among the best friends of my youth.

One remarkable thing in connection with the reception of the news of freedom by the slaves is the fact that the runaway slaves heard the news in time to come in and take part in the celebration. Runaway slaves that had been in the woods five years were celebrating on our place the next day. Two negroes, the property of Doctors Foster and Scales, who had enjoyed the freedom of the woods five years each, fat and sleek, were in to celebrate with the rest.

Before closing this article I must state that, owing to Master's kind manner of dealing with his slaves, no bloodhounds were allowed to be kept on the plantation. He regarded the chasing of slaves in that way as inhuman. When the overseer would attempt to show his superiority by wantonly picking a row with a slave, the latter would take to the woods till Master came, knowing that he would get the benefit of the doubt in Master's court. On that account our people were contemptuously referred to as "Edmond's free niggers." But the chasing of slaves with bloodhounds was an everyday occurrence in the swamps around our place until the war took the negro hunters in the front. I have witnessed many a thrilling chase, and sometimes a brutal capture. To tell of the means used by runaway slaves to fool the dogs would make this paper too long.

Since taking leave of my former master's family and my old fellow slaves I have had the honor to enjoy the personal acquaintance and confidence of Governors, United States Senators, Congressmen, and distinguished men and women in less-exalted walks of life: but I have never met nobler men and women than those composing the family that formerly owned me, and the slaves with whom I spent my early days.

To take from me the hope of meeting these dear old friends again in that blessed country where breathes no slave, is to deprive me of life's sweetest aspiration.

*

It took me years to be able to read through the entirety of this article. I'd read bits and pieces. I took breaks. I'd imagine what discussions he must have had with the editors at the *Los Angeles Times*: how he might have been asked to explain the "benefits" of slavery and what he "appreciated" about Master Edmonds and his children. We find Jefferson concerned about displeasing the Edmonds plantation owners, hesitating before signing the letter X on the contract that would have him and his family engaging in an exploitative sharecropping scheme on the Edmonds plantation. These were not sentiments he expressed in *The Liberator*. He rarely spoke of his personal accounts of the South or such colonized views of Africa. Instead he spoke of ending the cruel practice of lynchings, a lopsided educational system, and unfair housing in the South, but he didn't talk about his time on the plantation.

It always struck me that Jefferson wrote this piece for the *Los Angeles Times* and not in his own paper, *The Liberator*. I've spent a lot of time decoding the parts of this article meant for me, Black Angelenos, and what portions of his story were for the predominantly white readers at the *Times*. I imagined all the edits applied that would help shift the tone to appease *Los Angeles Times* readership. It took me down this rabbit hole of what we keep hidden and what we choose to expose; what we as Black people work out in the world as opposed to what we share in our living rooms and with our children and with our trusted friend circles. But that's for a future chapter—we'll find our way back to this later in the book.

Accompanying this article are written pieces from Allen Allensworth, best known for being a lieutenant colonel and chaplain for the American Army and the founder of the all-Black California city, Allensworth. This man, born enslaved in Kentucky, escaped slavery to fight for the Union in a voluntary infantry in the American Civil War. He, along with Booker T. Washington and Jefferson, used the word "savagery" to describe their African ancestry. They all discuss the benefits of forced labor and being enslaved as training for their success in America.

Some of these articles talked of the savagery of Africa and how the Holy Bible and Christianity saved their wretched souls. I've found it hard to believe that Jefferson, a man who ferociously fought for equal rights for his people and a safe place in the world, could have such dehumanizing views of his brothers, sisters, and ancestors living on the continent. In *The Liberator* we find Jefferson exploring his stance on Africa and the role Black Americans should hold in their native motherland.

> It has been fully 200 years since our ancestors left Africa, so we have lost track of whatever right or title to any property they may have held. No, we are an American of Americans, and feel a patriotic pride in our country. There are millions of negroes in this country that are going to stay here and the work of their uplift is so urgent that we can not desert them now. (*The Liberator* October 1910)

We see Jefferson distancing himself from the ideology around the Back to Africa movement led by Marcus Garvey, instead embracing this fight to preserve what had already been built by Black Americans. Over time, we'll see Jefferson questioning if his optimism and hope for a true Black American citizenship and all the rights and glory that comes with it was worth the fight in the end.

CHAPTER 2

Forging a Pathway for Liberation

The level of detail Jefferson shared in the 1909 *Los Angeles Daily Times* article to describe the day that he and his family learned of their freedom is completely astounding. The emotion he describes in each scene is absolutely palpable. Jefferson was born to be a journalist. He was bound to be a storyteller and a representative for all those who could not do it themselves. He may have had to keep his observations to himself and focus on his role as a farmer and teacher for the first half of his life, but he was always one to guard his rights and those of his community.

Jefferson's passion for documentation, preservation, and journalism had roots. Enslaved Africans arriving in the Americas and the Caribbean had to learn how to protect and hide information for safekeeping for generations. Just as they stored seeds of the provisions on the slave ships and eventually planted them for survival and memories of a far away home, so did Jefferson's Black press chart the same legacy and journey. Stories of Black triumph, connection, and family that had been documented and preserved in family Bibles and churches for years were finally brought to light and printed in newspapers like *The Liberator* to validate the Black American existence. This allowed for the Black Angeleno readership to bear witness to their glory and transformation from enslavement to Reconstruction, to a liberated life out west.

Recording our family lives in Bibles was our first step to prove our humanity and our first attempt to make a statement about our significance. We also began to keep public records in churches, transforming places of worship into collective memory centers for Black families to collect and retell their own living history. And then the Pullman train porters (discussed later in the book) gathered newsworthy information from white passengers traveling in first-class cars. The most compelling stories would be retold and reported in Black newspapers across the country. The same Pullman porters would also play a valuable role in helping to distribute Black newspapers along their train route. An elaborate underground network was created in an effort to help connect Black Southerners to the prospect of a new life up north.

The Holy Bible as the Recordkeeper

Before Black American citizenship rights were consecrated into constitutional law, they were documented primarily in personal ledgers and legal records dealing with property and plantation business management. Laws prohibited Black Americans from having birth, marriage, and death certificates, so family Bibles, passed down from generation to generation, served as a place to record life's transitions.

A 2002 oral history with Charles Blockson, preserved by the HistoryMakers Digital Archive, shares a common story of Black family recordkeeping.

> I came across the will of John Blockson. And then I started to read the will, and then he came across the name of Spencer Blockson. The name Spencer registered in my mind because in our family Bible, as I recall, it said Spencer died in his 70th year, but that's all I knew at the time. I found later on that my great-grandfather escaped in the Underground Railroad, came to Philadelphia, met with the great chronicler of the Underground Railroad, William Steele, an African American. And later other members of my family escaped and went to Canada. (Blockson 2002)

This beautiful discovery John Blockson speaks of shows the willpower and the perseverance needed to hold tight to Black American history—to hold it so tight that the next generation will never have to wonder. What a powerful example of how the family Bible has served as the verification needed to confirm lineage. For Black Americans, the Bible records oftentimes hold an even higher value than a legal document. Keeping records of our lives, our births, and our deaths became something that allowed our community to take back control. It was a form of resistance.

When the American legal system counted Black Americans as three-fifths of a person for electoral college votes, or when the names of our enslaved ancestors were documented on property insurance forms from companies like Aetna or New York Life, or on plantation bookkeeping ledgers in between crop production and farm equipment maintenance costs—we had the Bible. The Bible became the place where we would make sure to document our fullness and the wholeness of our existence.

The Black Church as the Sanctuary of History and Story

Black churches at the turn of the twentieth century proved to play a critical role in not only helping Black Americans develop new models of civic engagement and liberation strategies post-slavery, but in helping to establish their first museums, mini-repositories, and archives. The most powerful example is Mother Bethel African Methodist Episcopal (AME) Church, founded by Reverend Richard Allen in 1794 in Philadelphia, Pennsylvania (Dickerson 1983). Allen, a freedom fighter and social justice warrior in his time, became Bishop of AME. He, along with his spirited and brilliant wife, Sarah, led their congregation to invest fully in the abolitionist movement and support Black families and congregations around the nation in doing the same. Mother Bethel became one of the resting spots on the underground railroad and hosted honorable guests such as Frederick Douglass, Rosa Parks, and, later, Colin Powell (Howell 2009).

I was formally introduced to the Mother Bethel African Methodist Episcopal Church museum and archive while working on a project for the Historical Society of Pennsylvania back in 2008. I had attended several services at Mother Bethel over the years with my dear cousin Lauren, but never fully understood the history until this commissioned

Figure 2.1 Bishops of the AME Church, ca. 1876. Photograph by J. H. Daniels (Boston, MA). Library of Congress, https://www.loc.gov/itemt /98501269/.

documentary project. Along with a small film crew, I descended a long hallway and staircase to the basement, where the walls were lined with portraits of the head bishops and pastors over the years. I was there on a professional mission to share the untold histories of Philadelphia, but I found myself utterly speechless at the amount of stories, booklets, letters, photographs, deeds, and memorials dedicated to the church's involvement in liberation work in the City of Brotherly Love. The museum showcased the brave men and women who championed the abolition of slavery and secured a safe haven for Black Americans in the North, years before the Civil War.

In Los Angeles—the City of Angels—the First African Methodist Episcopal Church (First AME or FAME) was being constructed at the end of the nineteenth century. Much like Mother Bethel, the church mission was, and still is, rooted in Black liberation, civic engagement, and the spiritual well-being of fellow Black Angelenos. FAME would go on to document the early formation of the Black Angeleno community, and it became the centerpiece for major cultural shifts and a beacon of hope for Black families seeking refuge in the city (De Graaf et al. 2001).

The church was founded in 1872 by the famous Biddy Mason. The legend of Bridget "Biddy" Mason goes far beyond her critical leadership role at First AME. She was born enslaved in Mississippi in 1818. In 1848, Robert Marion Smith, her last owner, established a Mormon community in present-day Salt Lake City before forcing Mason and other enslaved caravan members to go to California to establish another Mormon post. Slavery was illegal in California at the time, and Mason, with the help of the Owens family, an established Black family in LA, was able to bring a case for her freedom from Smith to court. On January 21, 1856, LA District Judge Benjamin Hayes approved Mason's petition. The ruling freed Mason and thirteen members of her extended family (Reiniche 2023). Mason went on to become a midwife, open several orphanages, and support local churches, in the process becoming "one of the richest colored women west of the Mississippi Valley" (*The Liberator* March 1904). As former mayor of Los Angeles Meredith Snyder went on to note:

> Nearly twenty-three years ago it was my privilege to first meet Biddy Mason, or "Aunt Biddy," as we all loved to call her. . . . Her life was an effort for others. Like Biddy Mason, let us so order our conduct that people in contact with us may not forget us, and that our memories and deeds may shine forth as bright as the evening star. When we are called on to go hence and the tomb awaits these mortal bodies, then may our brothers and sisters say of us, as they say of her, "He was a good man; she was a good woman.
>
> (*The Liberator* March 1904)

While many biographies report on Mason's astute business acumen and her overflowing wealth and philanthropic giving, those who remembered her dearly almost always spoke of her kindness, her warmth, and her devotion to the people she loved. She set the standard and was an inspiration to so many early Black Angeleno pioneers then and today.

Jefferson had a way of highlighting the heroes of his time and making sure they received their due.

Attorney John W. Kemp shared at Mason's memorial "that the career of Biddy Mason was in many respects remarkable; and that, born enslaved, and hampered with many restrictions, she had succeeded in amassing a property that was valued at more than $100,000 [3.17 million today]. Yet it is not for this property, but her sweet, helpful Christian character that Biddy Mason is remembered" (*The Liberator* March 1904).

By the turn of the century First AME would become the headquarters for bustling social activity and civic training for the Black Angeleno community. In 1903, First AME became the birthplace for the Los Angeles Forum founded by Jefferson L. Edmonds, editor of *The Liberator*; the Reverend Jarrett E. Edwards, pastor of the First AME Church; and businessman John Wesley Coleman. The Forum was meant to be the first stop for newly arriving Black people to get resources about home ownership and setting up businesses, and to connect with fellow Angelenos. The Forum would go on to become a politically active organization that would instruct Black Angelenos on how to navigate civic life in the city (Jefferson et al. 2018).

Perhaps some of the most powerful contributions these AME churches provided the Black American community was intentional documentation, recordkeeping, and political organizing. This intentional work would prove to play a significant role in helping to shape Black American citizenship. When mainstream cultural institutions failed to prioritize the preservation of Black American histories and all their significant contributions to society, select AME churches around the nation would step in and preserve on their behalf.

AME churches founded at the turn of the century gave their members a place to reflect and build for a more secure future for Black Americans. These sanctuaries doubled as repositories and historical hubs that served as meeting spaces for voter engagement events, civic educational programing, and town halls for candidates running for office. Prospective candidates came before congregations nationwide to share their platform with ready and engaged Black citizens. These early civic events would help shape Black American citizenship, secure political power, and later guide Black Americans through the civil rights era. This turn-of-the-century political-building work at churches created the road map for Martin Luther King Jr. and his contemporaries in working with pastors and churches to share their message, of a just and equitable America. The speeches King gave in churches around the American South helped secure support for organizing sit-ins and protests in the 1960s.

Major moments in Black American history can trace their roots back to all the organizing that happened on church grounds. The church was at the center of Black citizenship (De Graaf et al. 2001). Often, the papers "borrowed printing presses from African American churches and soon the same machines that produced programs for Sunday services were printing the news" (Nelson 1999). Churches using their sacred space of worship to spark social movements, print the pages of Black newspapers to promote true Black liberation, and help define Black citizenship was visionary and future-focused.

Black Pullman Porters, Information Gatherers, and Distribution Networks

In the 1860s, railroad companies began expanding their routes, criss-crossing the continental United States. To support the train service expansion, railroad companies hired Pullman porters. George Pullman, a businessman and entrepreneur, began training and hiring formerly enslaved Black men to tend to the first-class white passengers with a neat and tidy appearance and a smile. This position was highly coveted within the Black community. The role offered newly freed Black men a chance to see the country, earn a steady paycheck to support family back home (although they were not always paid fair wages), and the opportunity to experience a type of freedom of movement they never experienced in their lives in bondage. While most passengers thought of these men as mere servants, many of these men moonlighted as journalists, collecting stories and important news of the day. Jefferson was one of them (Richardson 2016).

Even if the porters were considered to be subservient in their position as attendants, "aboard the nation's luxurious sleeper-train cars, the Pullman porter was an invisible man, privy to all manner of information. He was a clandestine news gatherer and subversive news distributor, often tossing black newspapers off their trains in between scheduled stops across the South" (Richardson 2016, 1–2). Many Pullman porters lived dual lives and "picked up tidbits about everything from politics to finances, and knew which to keep alive and which were privileged" (Richardson 2016, 7). According to Larry Tye's book *Rising from the Rails*, Pullman porters not only gathered important news stories, but would later play an integral role in the distribution of Black newspapers across the South (Tye 2004). Robert Abbott, founder and editor of the *Chicago Defender*, dedicated his newspaper to encouraging Black Americans to leave the South and journey northbound to Chicago for a better way of living. In the early 1900s, after the dust of the Reconstruction era had settled and sharecropping was in full swing, Southern politicians didn't want to lose their poorly paid workforce. These politicians not only discouraged the reading and distribution of Black newspapers, but also made concerted efforts to prevent Black families from gaining access to the world outside of the South.

Abbott knew his papers still needed to reach the South. Journalism professor Patrick Washburn explained in 1999 in the award-winning PBS documentary *The Black Press: Soldiers without Swords* that Abbott distributed his paper by going

> out to the railroad yards to one of the most distinguished professions in the black community at that time, the sleeping car porters and he hands them bundles of his newspapers, which they hide in the train, and as these trains roll through the South, instead of being put off at the stations like they used to be, which are in the town limits or the city limits, these porters would step out between cars or at the back of the train, toss 'em out in the countryside and suddenly all these Southern cities found they couldn't stop the Black newspapers, no matter what they did. (Nelson 1999)

*

Back in 2009, I interviewed my great-aunt Evelyn Osborne, Jefferson's granddaughter, about what she remembered of her grandfather. She was in her eighties at the time, frail and starting to lose some of her mobility. She sat propped up in her wheelchair with her signature neutral-toned, thick-rimmed glasses and very short, cropped afro. She was getting older but was still spicy and still firm, just as she'd been during her years as a principal for Los Angeles Unified School District.

Together we sat in her living room, and among her beautifully crafted quilts and handmade crochet throws, we talked about Jefferson. She grinned and asked why I wanted to know so much about him. I told her my dad got me interested, and once my cousin Dawson had sent me a census record from 1900 with Jefferson's name, I began wondering about his kids and his personal life. He died well before my great-aunt Evelyn was born, but stories of his life and legacy had been passed down generation after generation. She talked about his involvement with the founders of the NAACP, and how his farm grew some of the best greens, but what stood out was how he'd gotten to LA in the first place. Jefferson was a Pullman porter and worked on the trains from the late 1880s to the early 1890s, and he used his time on the trains to learn about the American West and earn enough money to have his family relocate to Los Angeles.

I began imagining him in his uniform, with a pleasant welcoming spirit greeting the all-white guests as they arrived on the first-class dining cars. I thought about him as a young boy on the Edmonds Plantation, where he was advised not to share with friends and family the things he saw while completing tasks as an errand boy in the city center. He had already lived a life with small windows into a foreign forbidden world. As Jefferson wrote in his 1909 *Los Angeles Daily Times* article, "I lived in a new atmosphere . . . I had seen wonders, but for want of words my tongue was still. I couldn't tell anything" (Edmonds 1909).

Jefferson would travel back and forth on the trains—saving, greeting, serving, invisible. It would be the prelude to a new life. A life where he wouldn't have to keep quiet. Where he could scream, shout, and proclaim something bigger, something he could call his own.

PART II

What Brought Us Together

A Migration Story

> It's very hard to sit at a typewriter and concentrate on [your work] if you're afraid of the world around you. The years I lived in Paris did one thing for me, they released me from that particular social terror which was not the paranoia of my own mind, but a real social danger visible in the face of every cop, every boss, everybody.
> —James Baldwin, interview with Paul Wiess on *The Dick Cavett Show*, May 16, 1969

I felt that statement in my body. So I wrapped up Baldwin's words in my breast pocket near my heart and left LA in the winter of 2020.

I didn't bring much with me: just a suitcase, my round, moon-shaped black patent leather 1960s carry-on, mostly filled with books, scrap papers, and a photo of my Aunt Selena who had passed away a few years back. I had about eight bold-patterned outfits, one big-brimmed hat, a few pairs of cat-eye sunglasses that I would rotate throughout the weeks—my uniforms, as my friend Anwar would call them. And that was it. I didn't do much research about all the places I wanted to visit while I was on my trip. I came by faith and was led by spirit. I trusted the friends I was traveling with. The people who knew the continent, knew West Africa, and could help me navigate this new world.

I landed in Dakar on Sunday. The melodic sound of Wolof and French swirled around me, and I couldn't find the *toilettes*. My friend Anwar met me at the airport. We jumped in his rented, beat-up Mitsubishi gray truck with the busted taillight and drove to the Radisson Blu hotel to get breakfast. We also went to show off our carefully curated outfits, take a few photos, and get some money out of the ATM. What was meant to be a forty-minute stop ended up in a downward spiral with my bank card being eaten by the machine and a two-day episode with hotel management in English and French trying to get it back. Finally, we would settle in our new spot overlooking the Atlantic Ocean with a grand view of the 161-foot-tall bronze Monument de la Renaissance Africaine depicting the strength of the African family, *Assalamu alaikum, wa-alaikum-salaam*, we'd chant, as we flowed in and out of our building and greeted the front doormen.

Later in the week, I would sit for hours with my friend Brittanie as we got our hair braided past our hips. In this garage-turned-hair-salon, we'd watch Spanish soap operas dubbed in French, pick the bones out of the fish in our Thieboudienne, and smile politely because my French— Oh Lord, my French, is nonexistent. Several hours in, a woman walked into the salon. Her face looked like my Aunt Nana's. My Nana comes back to say hello in the form of white butterflies everywhere I go. Perhaps she'd sent the butterflies and the woman with the baby slung on her back to remind me that I'm never alone. That she is always with me and that I was ready for a new start.

Our trio wandered over to Ghana the following month. I didn't have an end plan. All I knew was that I had to go. My research about Black Angelenos over the years was centered on all the effort and all the strategies used to help create a new world in the West. A world that would be vastly different from the violent South so many of them had escaped.

Ghana became the place where I would build my new life. Much like all the Black families Jefferson urged to come to California, my friend Allen and his family welcomed me with open arms. They took me in during the middle of a pandemic, where social uprisings were in full force, and I couldn't breathe or concentrate or sleep. They showed me that

my life on the continent could be full and loving and free. I was supported through friends and later family on how to best navigate life in
Ghana. They showed me how to invest in businesses, purchase land, and
most importantly how to work and grow within the community. Things
weren't perfect when I landed on the continent. There was a lot of learning and unlearning that took place as I started rebuilding my new life.
Looking back, the biggest gift and lesson I received was the realization
that life is not meant to be weathered alone. I understood that concept
intellectually. I understood the concept through my research of all the
community and political organizing Jefferson did in his lifetime. But
Ghana gave me the chance to embody the concepts of interdependency,
belonging, and true community-building.

I stepped into the shoes of those early Black Angeleno settlers and
experienced the dedication and love Jefferson once extended to so many.
I can only imagine how vulnerable and terrifying it must have been for
the newly arriving Angelenos. What tremendous courage it took for
those early settlers to start over in a new place, all while still recovering
from the violence and discrimination of the South. They, just like me,
were seeking peace, a way to invest and prosper in a new land where they
could breathe and just be.

Jefferson knew that as he invited Black families to join him in LA they
would need not only housing, jobs, and community, but they'd need a
record of their lives. They would need a newspaper! A paper that would
help guide them throughout their new journey. Just as I jotted notes in
my journal and created the record of my travels on the continent to help
ground me, Jefferson created a public memory portal with *The Liberator* and affirmed the burgeoning Black Angeleno community: *I see you.
You're not alone on this journey. You've been given everything you need. We
will do this together.*

Daddy

Daddy,

You've held steady on this journey with me. We did it together. When I wanted to jump ahead and say yes to a shiny new opportunity you encouraged me to think about Jefferson's vision first. If I'm the spokesperson, the one out front doing the workshops, interviews, and panels that add to the collective memory of Angeleno history, then you were the original keeper. You held steady until I was ready to take on this role. The one who would evaluate if the next move was aligned. The one who would protect, inform, and guide our path. Jefferson handed the papers down to Aunt Susie, then to Grandpa, and from Grandpa to you. Instead of waiting until your last days to start sharing these LA histories, you had the foresight to start dropping hints in my teenage years. "Together," you'd say, "we will work on a project that will make a difference in people's lives." It was easy to shrug it off. But thank you for never letting go. Thank you for being the light and my inspiration along the way. None of this could have happened without you. Thank you.

CHAPTER 3

No Longer Will Others Speak for Us

We find Jefferson again in the records at a teaching college in Columbus, Mississippi, in April of 1875. He'd left the town where the Edmonds Plantation operated around 1873. Several historical accounts show that Jefferson learned to read and write through the Freedom Bureau Schools, an initiative created during the Reconstruction era (1865–1877), a time of rebuilding and acclimation for Black citizenry after the turbulence and terror of the Civil War. The Reconstruction era provided a pathway to a different life for newly freed enslaved people. Major strides and achievements happened during that short decade—but these advancements came with much opposition and violence.

After the passing, in February 1870, of the 15th Amendment, which granted Black men the right to vote, dozens of congressional Black leaders began springing out of the South. Jefferson became a part of that sweeping change by his political organizing work and canvassing in Clay County, Mississippi, in the mid-1870s. He most likely was backing Republican senate candidate Blanche K. Bruce's campaign in 1875. Rising fear among white Southern leadership led to the formation of the "Mississippi Plan" in 1890. The plan included several provisions intended to suppress the Black vote by requiring a poll tax, a literacy test, and specific residency requirements, all in efforts to legally deter organized Black power in the South (Sharpe et al. 2001).

As Jefferson traveled around Clay County giving speeches and encouraging Black men to vote, his efforts were met with threats and violence from angry mobs.

Jefferson was summoned to testify before members of the US Senate in a hearing to investigate voter suppression and violence in Mississippi's 1875 election. He was interviewed by Senator George Boutwell, one of the coauthors of the 14th and 15th Amendments. Below is a transcription of the 1875 Senate hearing:

> Q: Did you know anything about the election canvas of last year? If you do, you can state to the committee what you know.
>
> A: I went around a great deal in the county in the Republican canvas, and I spoke, I think, a time or two in the last campaign. I continued to go to them until I was attacked in the streets of West Point one day by a man by the name of McCeachin. He attacked me on the street. There were four or five with him, and asked "why I was going around speaking, what did I have to do with it?" I told him just because I belonged to the party. He told me, "I want you to stop and have no more to do with it," or they would kill me. They had pistols in their hands and were armed. I had to make the promise to save my life; and then they let me loose . . . [they] attacked me again, and told me, if I ever went around making speeches anywhere in the country to put on my burying clothes, as I would never come back to West Point any more. (Boutwell June 26, 1876, 234)

Jefferson goes on to mention that to get ballot tickets to prepare for the election was nearly impossible, because white Democratic leaders were stationed outside of the clerk's office all day and all night. He mentions how dangerous it was for him to travel at night through the woods to get ballot information.

Nearly three decades later Jefferson would go on to print voter ballots on the front pages of *The Liberator* for all to have access—for all to have a fair advantage. At the turn of the century Jefferson would again report on intimidation tactics used by "political amateurs" during an important Los Angeles mayoral race in the winter of 1902. He shared that putting a bloody garment at the top of the *Los Angeles Times* building or in Black neighborhoods to deter voting was tired and played out: "These fledglings will yet learn that *The Liberator* has made the bloody shirt useless as a political argument, by teaching the colored voters to think, O yes, that old garment may stampeed the steers in Texas, but won't frighten them here" (*The Liberator* December 1902). I'm sure his twenty-four-year-old self would have been amazed and proud to have endured so much, fought with such vigor, and yet still managed to pave a way for Black citizenship rights, on his own terms.

Jefferson's testimony continues, as he shares with the committee that these white Southern Democrats were not just issuing out idle threats:

> They would take a cannon and load it up with chains and leave it with the mouth pointing toward the crowd of colored people. When they fired they had nothing in it more than powder, but when they were going to speak they would have it turned around and chains hanging around it.
>
> They had a parade at West Point. I was standing on the corner talking and some of the colored men came up, and a colored man says, "I do not care how many are riding around, I am a Republican and expect to vote the ticket." Just then a man walked up with a pistol and shot him. Pretty soon another colored man made some expression and he was shot at.
>
> They had flags—red, white, and crimson flags. The whole street was covered. You could not hear your ears hardly for the flags waving and flapping over your head. They had one United States [flag] at the courthouse but most of the flags were just the old Confederate flags.
>
> They said they were going to beat at this election. They said that at the meetings, on the stumps and at school houses around the county. They said they would carry the county or kill every nigger. They would carry it if they had to wade in blood. (Boutwell June 26, 1876, 234)

This section of Jefferson's testimony is a glimpse into the beginning of his life as a civil servant and freedom fighter, and his fraught relationship with the United States government and the amendments meant to protect its citizens. Jefferson was courageous enough to speak truth to power. One of the very people who amended the constitution of the United States, which allowed Jefferson the ability to vote, stood before him and Jefferson bravely faced him to say, *"I'm being punished for exercising my new citizenship rights. My life is in danger."*

The strength needed to speak so openly, so freely. This testimony set the stage for the many challenges that Jefferson would take on in his lifetime. He would stay in Mississippi another fifteen years to teach in the public school system—but his commitment and dedication to educating Black people would be a lifetime appointment. Disseminating important information regarding safety and prosperity for Black Americans would be a focal point of every entrepreneurial pursuit in Jeffersons's life. It all started in Mississippi.

For me, it all started in Pasadena, when my mom and I would volunteer at the NAACP office a few times a month. I'd watch how the chapter president would listen intently to each and every person who walked in the door. He became a witness to anyone filing a complaint about discrimination or race-based violence. He sat with them, empathized with them. I saw firsthand the power of telling your story, seeking help, advocating for yourself and your community. Years later, in the fall of 2021, I would get the chance to speak up and advocate for our community just as my mom's colleagues at the NAACP had done, and just as Jefferson stood before US elected officials and proclaimed his truth.

California Governor Gavin Newsom created the first-in-the nation Reparations Task Force. It was made up of appointed committee members and California elected officials charged with working with the Department of Justice to listen to key witnesses, hold town hall sessions, and research the effect of slavery in America. They were asked to submit a report in 2023 with recommendations on policies for reparations efforts for descendants of enslaved Africans in America. I was selected as one of the key experts. Just like Jefferson, I stood before a senate council and shared all the ways Black Americans are still facing disenfranchisement, discrimination, and are unable to fully exercise our rights as citizens. I was pregnant with my daughter at the time, and I was feeling both humbled and empowered by the opportunity to stand in Jefferson's shoes almost 150 years later. I put on my red power suit and a red lip and shared the following:

> Our world broke open after George Floyd and the start of the pandemic, and, as a result, we've been given an opening, a portal to re-examine ourselves, our past and make decisions about how this nation will approach repair and reparations for Black Americans. Co-creating reparations policies is a complex exercise. In part because the exploitation of Black American labor for hundreds of years is in direct correlation with America transforming into the global superpower we know today. A lot of

unfolding and reckoning is necessary for the restoration work to be done right.

It's my theory that when dealing with complicated, painful, and deeply rooted issues, strategizing and applying intellectual frameworks can only take us so far. Stories of our human experience and the things that tie us together have proven over and over to provide the keys to unlock the most challenging issues we've faced in our history. So today I'd like to introduce you to my great-great-grandfather Jefferson Lewis Edmonds, a formerly enslaved man turned newspaper editor, farmer, and civil rights advocate who dedicated his life to his family, his community, and the advancement of a fulfilled Black American life. You'll hear about Jefferson using his newspaper, *The Liberator*, as a platform to combat local and national government policies engineered to restrict Black American rights and our ability to freely exercise our citizenship. As I share Jefferson's story, I'm asking the committee members to bear in mind that many of the battles Jefferson tackled in his paper over 120 years ago are the same issues we face today. How might we learn from his story as we approach this historical moment of national reparations? (Edmonds 2021)

The Transition to Print

In 1890, Jefferson started purchasing land near Mississippi, about thirty-five miles south of Memphis, Tennessee. The *California Eagle* shared in a retrospective of Jefferson that on his land were hickory, walnut, and cypress trees used for lumber and that his farms produced "some of the finest cotton, corn and potatoes in the state." But farming life wasn't enough for him. He fixed his eyes westward, and by 1893 Jefferson started preparing for his second act—his life as a newspaper man. I can't help but imagine that if he was reading William Lloyd Garrison's *Liberator* papers, he must have been aware of and inspired by John Brown Russwurm and Samuel Cornish. They were the owners and coeditors of America's first Black newspaper, *Freedom's Journal*, founded in 1827. These editors declared in their first edition, "We wish to plead our own cause. Too long have others spoken for us" (*Freedom's Journal*, March 16, 1827).

According to author Winston James, "Cornish and Russwurm saw *Freedom's Journal* as an organizer; they sought to meld the scattered Black population in the United States into one people, with the *Journal* as its advocate and articulate voice" (James 2010, 28). The paper made clear efforts to mobilize Black Americans and condemn those who sought to uphold the brutal system of American slavery. These values seemed to propel the work of the abolitionist movement, a movement that Jefferson later modeled when helping to secure civil rights for free Black Americans at the turn of the century.

Attempts at Stifling Progress

At the close of the Reconstruction era, Black elected officials began filling more and more seats in Washington; what are now known as Historically Black Colleges and Universities were being erected across the country; and the Black press was starting to make headway and pick up steam. Then in 1892, activist and prolific writer Ida B. Wells, editor and founder of the newspaper *The Memphis Free Speech*, faced an angry mob who destroyed her printing press office. Wells's anti-lynching articles cut to the very core of race issues in America, and her sharp wit and unrelenting commentary made her a threat for white Southerners trying to maintain their oppressive regime. (Nelson 1999). According to historian Jane Rhodes, interviewed in the film *The Black Press*:

> She really set the stage for a very radical, very activist kind of black journalism. And as a black woman, she was also an inspiration because there were so few African American women who had worked in journalism before. And when they did, it tended to be sort of a social service-oriented journalism, not the sort of powerful, radical, you know, vociferous journalism that said, "We won't stand for this. We must do something about the kinds of violence affecting African Americans."

Six years after the unfortunate loss of the *Memphis Free Speech* headquarters, in North Carolina the Wilmington Massacre of 1898 erupted and led to the killing of hundreds of Black citizens and the burning of the printing offices of Alexander and Frank Manly, founders and editors of Wilmington's *Daily Record.* In a bold op-ed that caused upset and retaliation from white residents, editor Frank Manly openly condemned white supremacists who advocated for lynchings (Neuman 2021).

The free Black press was dangerous for Southern Democratic leaders at the turn of the twentieth century. The words being printed in these turn-of-the-century Black newspapers were creating an awakening among Black America, and this triggered efforts to squelch advancement of Black liberation movements by white Southern political leaders. Former plantation owners who relied on exploitative sharecropping schemes feared losing their cheap labor force due to the Black press encouraging migration out of the South. These radical ideals in the Black press spread like wildfire, leading to hundreds of thousands leaving the South to seek better living conditions all across the county.

White Southern political leaders made attempts to reroute Black newspapers being delivered from places like Chicago or New York or Los Angeles (Nelson 1999). Despite their multiple attempts to destroy the Black press, by 1900 more than 500 Black newspapers were being published in cities like Omaha, Mobile, Indianapolis, Cleveland, and San Francisco, and in smaller towns like Galveston, Texas; Coffeeville, Kansas; and Langston City, Oklahoma Territory. The efforts to shut down the free Black press created the opposite effect—Black American writers and journalists had something to share, and not much could stop them (Nelson 1999)!

Long gone were the days when enslaved men and women were escaping plantations on the underground railroad, coding their next moves and directions in songs. No more were Black families willing to stay in the South and suffer under oppressive Jim Crow laws; they were ready for a life worth living. They were ready for a freedom that didn't ask them to wait for heaven.

Jefferson was one of those writers who was longing for something more. With all the painful experiences of discrimination, threats of violence, and violations of his civil rights, he still moved westward and turned his attention to text, the written word. Perhaps his political canvassing, teaching, and yearning for a more civilly engaged life couldn't be fulfilled in the American South. Perhaps his testimony sparked a fire in him to continue to tell his story and the story of Black people around the nation. Perhaps much like Baldwin's escape to Paris, and my trek to Ghana, he too went to LA for more inspiration and less fear. A place where he could tell his own story.

CHAPTER 4

Jefferson in Los Angeles

With great faith, Jefferson and his two colleagues, L. C. Young and L. A. Bell, left Hollywood, Mississippi, by train heading westbound on a six-day journey to Los Angeles on December 29, 1892. Jefferson's wife, Ida, and their nine kids (Jefferson Jr., Garfield, Susie, Ida Jr., Cordilla, Blanchard, Walter, Sallie, and Willie—Lena would be born in April of 1897) would join him a few months later in March of 1893 (*California Eagle*, December 18, 1941). They settled in Pasadena, California, and Jefferson hit the ground running. By 1895, he'd purchased a farm in South Pasadena, and by 1896 he collaborated with the Reverend S. S. Freeman, William Prince, and H. H. Williams to launch the *Pasadena Searchlight* newspaper. Jefferson was selected as editor, and he became heavily involved in political organizing for the presidential election of 1896, Williams Jennings Bryan versus William McKinley. What was unique about this election was that the country was divided on the issue of gold-backed currency versus silver money. This was a high-priority topic for most voting Americans at the time. Jefferson sided with the farmers, who backed the silver currency. They were championed by the charismatic Democratic leader Bryan, who ran on the platform that farmers debt relief and currency inflation would help economic growth.

Being a farmer himself, Jefferson crossed party lines to endorse Bryan's campaign. His dedication earned him a seat on the Executive Committee of the Silver Republican Party of Los Angeles County in 1898. The following year, Jefferson began serving on the Executive Committee for the Negro National Democratic League and traveled to Kansas for the Sixth Biennial Session in support of the Bryan/Stevenson nomination. The only challenge Jefferson faced was that most Black voters at the time were loyal to the Republican Party, the party of Lincoln, the "Great Emancipator." Jefferson's views and backing of Bryan were experimental and nontraditional for the time. Below is an excerpt from a retrospective Jefferson wrote sixteen years later, in a November 15th, 1912, article about his time as editor of *The Liberator* and his foresight into issue-based voting.

I'll let Jefferson explain:

> Having reached the conclusion that the political ills of the Negroes were due to the fact that they voted solidly for one party regardless of issues, and that such voting was dangerous not only to the voters themselves, but to the community in which such voters reside, we made up our mind to publish a newspaper advocating a division of the Negro vote.
>
> In 1896, we commenced the publication of *The Searchlight*, a weekly paper. In the municipal campaign of that year we supported the Democratic ticket headed by Hon. M. P. Snyder for mayor. We took the position that the city government ought to be non-partisan, and that its officers should be selected only on the ground of fitness; and all city officers would have to be taken out of partisan politics.

Jefferson's stance on nonpartisan policy was ahead of its time; we'll find that his views were adopted by local government officials over a decade later. However, back in the late 1890s, *The Searchlight* stakeholders began to demand that the issue-based, democratic-leaning platform of the periodical change directions, claiming it was not in the best interest of the Black community. Jefferson was criticized by Black community leaders who "by fives and tens, each week ordered the paper stopped. 'I want no Democratic paper in my house,' accompanied every request to stop the paper" (November 15, 1912).

Jefferson wouldn't budge, and by 1898 he was ousted as editor of the *The Searchlight* and denounced by Black political leaders of the time. He dug his heels in further when asked to pen a political opinion piece for the October 16, 1898 Sunday edition of the *Los Angeles Herald* on the subject "Why are the colored voters supporting the union ticket?"

Jefferson's sharp-witted opening line states plainly: "This question might be succinctly answered by saying: They have been reading, they are thinking." He goes on to say that "those who denounce us as traitors and bribe takers for attempting to exercise these rights are not as loyal to their country as its interests demand."

> The grand old Republican party, with its divine ambitions and immortal leaders, has gone over the auction block route into the coffers of corporate greed and scrabble for place. Upon the ruins of the grand old party's auspicious beginning and magnificent career stands the altar of the golden calf of the party today.
>
> We are beginning to regard ourselves as American citizens as no longer scullions of the Republican Party. [no longer] leaving the party to do our thinking.
>
> American citizenship with us today means the right to think and act for ourselves; to vote as our interest dictates; to vote for men and measures instead of party. We have learned that no slave is so universally despised as the party slave; that no slave can be an American citizen in the full sense of that term.

At the tipping point of the twentieth century and in the middle of the chaos, ousted from his community, deemed a traitor and a heretic, Jefferson once again directed his gaze westward and moved his operations and ideology to 616 South Broadway Street in downtown Los Angeles. It would be in the City of Angels where Jefferson would continue honing his stance on issue-based voting, civic engagement, and Black American citizenship as a tool for advancement from the shackles of an enslaved mindset. "We kept up the agitation unceasingly" (*The Liberator* November 15, 1912) Jefferson wrote in reference to the importance of having a strong unified Black vote. With that bold declaration, Jefferson turned the page and entered a new century, a new chapter: "Realizing the power of the press as a molder of sentiment, we began publishing *The Liberator* in 1900" (*The Liberator* November 15, 1912).

The Liberator Origins

There are two theories on how Jefferson got the name for his new paper. Perhaps the most obvious—and the one Jefferson was vocal about— was that his paper was an ode to William Lloyd Garrison, the revered abolitionist and newspaper editor of the original *Liberator*, established on January 1, 1831. It's my hunch that abolitionist and revolutionary John Brown's children may have played more of an inspiration for the paper's name.

On January 9, 1889, prior to Jefferson stepping into his role as editor of the *Pasadena Searchlight*, the great abolitionist Owen Brown passed away. Over 2,000 mourners, Black and white alike, participated in a procession toward the Altadena Mountains to pay their respects to the son of John Brown. The tombstone read in block letters, similar to the typeface used on the pages of our family newspaper: "Owen Brown, Hero and Son of John Brown 'THE LIBERATOR'" (Lindahl 2019).

Owen Brown had joined his father in the pre–Civil War raid in Harpers Ferry, Virginia, on October 16, 1859, in an attempt to eradicate slavery in the US. While John Brown was executed on charges of treason, murder, and insurrection, his son Owen was able to escape and found safety in the mountains of Altadena, just north of Pasadena. Here he would live out the rest of his days (Lindahl 2019). Jefferson befriended the Brown family while living in Pasadena. He used the paper and his connections with local church groups to advocate for John Brown's eldest daughter, Ruth Brown Thompson, when she fell ill and she and her husband faced financial troubles with their estate. As the paper declared, "The sacrifices John Brown made for the freedom of the slaves are well known and appreciated by all. Mr. Thompson, his son-in-law, who is now 79 years old, was a soldier in Captain Brown's ranks when he was fighting battles for liberty. In his youth he fought for us; now that he is old shall we forget him?" (*The Liberator* June 1901). Jefferson, along with longtime collaborator and friend the Reverend E. J. Edwards, would speak at Ruth Brown Thompson's memorial service:

> Her childhood home was a cradle of a heroic agitation against the sin of slavery; and from it went forth a stalwart spirit to battle against human bondage. At her father's fireside the fugitive slave found that warmth and welcome that help and hope sanctioned by Holy writ The Bible and which defied the cruel decrease of corrupt courts.
>
> (*Los Angeles Times* January 25, 1904)

Jefferson's reverence for abolitionists like Douglass, Brown, and Garrison, who dedicated their lives to freedom and fairness, is what gave our family paper its namesake. Each article, each poem, each fiery op-ed about international policy or cruel Southern politics harks back to Jefferson's deep humility that he once lived his life in bondage and that due to the efforts of the liberators who came before him, he could use his voice to shout:

> We are proud of the negro race and its achievements, proud of its religious fervor and virtuous tendencies, proud to be a member of the race, that in spite of its unparalleled trials and tribulations produced Frederick Douglass and Booker T. Washington.
>
> (*The Liberator* January 1904)

Political Organizing

Within the first few years of arriving in California, Jefferson joined the Afro-American Council, a national network originally formed to combat the nation's failure to uphold the 14th and 15th Amendments. In 1895, the California local league held their annual conference in San Francisco to establish their statewide African American League. The group was addressed by the mayor and garnered financial support from *Los Angeles Times* owner Harris Grey Otis. Among some of the early, exclusively male members was editor of the *Eagle* newspaper, John Neimore; John Wesley Coleman (Jefferson's cofounder for the LA Forum); and T. A. Green, all of whom would work side-by-side with Jefferson in a pursuit for a more equitable Los Angeles. Jefferson's involvement would help to set the tone for his civic leadership at the LA Forum, an organization that admitted women and men (Flamming 2005).

Jefferson's civic efforts were not focused squarely on *The Liberator* and reporting to the community. He engaged in campaigns to protect Black American civil rights all over the nation. One notable campaign was the unjust discharge of the Buffalo Soldiers of the 25th Infantry Regiment at Fort Brown in Brownsville, Texas, in 1906. With mounting tension between the townspeople and the troops, the regiment was accused of murdering a white bartender and wounding a white police officer, despite reports from army commanders affirming that the soldiers had been in the barracks all evening and not at the scene (Wormser et al. 2002).

After a military investigation, President Theodore Roosevelt ordered that 167 soldiers of the 25th Infantry Regiment be discharged without honor or a trial. The discharge on the account of "conspiracy of silence" resulted in the soldiers losing their pensions and being barred from government civil service opportunities (Foner 1974, 98). This issue rolled over to the Taft presidential campaign two years later, because Taft was serving as secretary of war, and it was his office that recommended the discharge. Black freedom fighters and political activists all over the nation orchestrated protests, rallies, and political interference to address the injustice; Jefferson took the lead in Los Angeles. He started a committee to organize the LA-based protests and help secure a list of heavy-hitter speakers (*Los Angeles Herald* May 31, 1908).

The continued pressure resulted in several of the soldiers being allowed to reenlist. However, it would be nearly seventy years later when all but one soldier, Dorsie Willis, was still alive, that the United States government, under Nixon's administration, would pardon and restore the Buffalo Soldiers' records to show honorable discharges. To date, no retroactive compensation has been paid out to the families of the 25th Infantry Regiment (Lembeck 2015).

The Platform

Gracing the front page of every edition of *The Liberator* is the motto "Devoted to the Cause of Good Government and the Advancement of the Afro-American." And the paper did just that. Over its fourteen-year span the paper covered a myriad of issues, from gender equality to land ownership, education, and racial upliftment. Jefferson advocated for the Women's Suffrage Movement nearly a decade before the 19th

Amendment was added to the United States Constitution, and he urged African Americans to join in support. *The Liberator* was used to reshape the narrative about Black life by depicting Los Angeles as a beautiful haven for formerly enslaved people, redefining what it meant to be seen as American citizens.

The Promise

Throughout the paper, Jefferson discusses the importance of not just owning land to survive but owning land and benefiting from its highest value. On the front page of his April 12, 1912, edition he shared that the chief value of a California farm "depends more upon the safety of life than the fertility of the soil. Where life isn't safe, property is without value." He's illustrating something very powerful and nuanced in these few opening lines—something that I believe makes Jefferson stand out among his newspaper editor contemporaries. He's working from the assumption that these formerly enslaved people already see the value of owning land. They already understand that being profitable and having control over your destiny is vital for survival in America. At this time we might still find articles in Black newspapers around the country instructing formerly enslaved people how to comb their hair and look presentable in major cities. Jefferson spoke to his readers' highest selves. He spoke to their future selves, and he spoke to the dreams they had for their children and their children's children.

He not only preached the words of land ownership and entrepreneurship—he lived it. After his transition from the *Pasadena Searchlight* in the late 1890s, Jefferson prepared for yet another big move. In May of 1902, he sold his farm in South Pasadena and purchased five acres of commercial farmland on the corner of Minnesota and Fourteenth Street in Sawtelle, a neighborhood situated between Santa Monica and Culver City, not far from the ocean (*Los Angeles Times* May 12, 1902). He continued to cultivate his agricultural calling from the farms he owned and operated in Mississippi to his farmland in South Pasadena, to his final resting place in Sawtelle.

The young errand boy from the Edmonds Plantation who had been told to not share what he saw when walking down the main road in the city center had been transformed. The boy who had access and information he was forced to keep hidden from those around him became the man who dedicated his life to doing the exact opposite. He shouted from the rooftops for anyone who would hear—*This life could be glorious. We can have a life that could be fulfilling and powerful.*

Jefferson was more than a Los Angeles booster encouraging Black Southerners to escape; he was asking his fellow and future Black Angelenos to dream. To imagine a place where generational success, fulfillment, and support didn't have to exist hand-in-hand with suffering, devastation, and fear. He invited Black families to come and live a life of wonder. One might read through these articles and find a man advocating for a mass exodus from the South to Los Angeles for better living conditions. He pushed for those potentially relocating to enroll their children in the local high school in their community, pointing out that large cities offer "Polytechnic Schools where the farmer's boys can learn the trades free and those who are unable to attend in the day schools can enter the night classes, which are also free" (*The Liberator* April 12, 1912).

Jefferson's fifteen years as a Mississippi public school teacher (which he discussed in *The Liberator*'s January 10, 1913, edition) shines through quite a bit in his approach to editing. He often stressed to his readers that understanding our collective past and investing in education is the only doorway to citizenship and success. He would often give mini history lessons and tools on how to place oneself in the American timeline and grab ahold of all the good parts:

> Amid this jungle of conflicting prejudice the negro paused in his phantom- like chase for political greatness and realized that he had yet to fit himself for the duties and responsibilities of life, and qualify for the eminence of American citizenship. The negro realized that he needed education. With the realization of this truth he had found the key that would unlock the door of prejudice and uproot the sprouts of hatred that had been planted.
>
> When in the early '70s this idea of education had become generally a set desire, there arose from the humble log cabins of the American negroes

such a hustle, and actual activity to accomplish their desires for culture as have never been put forth by any people in the history of the world. They were the days of the Freedmen's Bureau, the old blue-back spelling book, the spelling match; the days of the barefooted boy and girl, with a zeal and determination to learn something; the days of pine-knots, that furnished light for the little groups of poorly clad students by night; these were the days when God had come to lift and guide with His own strong hand a much neglected and persecuted people.

In a short time method and system found a place in the conduct of the education of the young negro. School houses began springing up here and there, and the negro took advantage of every opportunity that was offered. After the common school of the olden time came the graded school. Then there was a demand for higher education, which was met by the erection of such schools as Hampton, Fisk and Howard Universities. Today the negro is proud of some of the best Normal schools and colleges in America. He has twenty-seven thousand school teachers, one thousand lawyers, two thousand physicians, and a host of educated men and women fitted for other spheres in life.

(*The Liberator* September 1901)

When I read articles like these I hear Jefferson saying, *Yes, come to LA for education, the land, and a new future. But also, brothers and sisters, be ready to leave a life of enslavement and servitude and trust me it will be transformational.* He asked them to trust that they could do everything they'd done in the South but this time not as unworthy second-class citizens. He invited tens of thousands of Black people who would eventually migrate in the 1920s and 1930s—LA's biggest migration period (Bunch 2001)—to take hold of a promised land—like the slaves escaping Egypt (Bunch 2001)—where their children and all the untapped growth that lay just beneath the surface of their imagination could take full bloom.

The words dancing across the pages of *The Liberator* feel like prayers, mantras, and spiritual text dipped in a promise that life could be more. Just as Shug Avery from *The Color Purple* said, "I think it pisses God off if you walk by the color purple in a field somewhere and don't notice it. People think pleasing God is all God cares about. But any fool living in the world can see it always trying to please us back" (Walker 1982, 178).

The Man Behind the Press

I spent so many years trying to piece together Jefferson's legacy and all of his achievements. I wanted to build him up as a hero, a champion, untouchable even. I wanted to show all the ways he'd influenced the formation of the Black Angeleno community. I was so focused on his efforts, his legacy. However, in recent years, after the birth of my daughter, I started to understand what fueled Jefferson's work—it was family.

Jefferson put his kids on several cover pages of *The Liberator*, and he ran ads for their businesses and celebrated when they achieved high marks in school or won competitions. He wrote about their graduations and their dreams and his grandkids. He let his readership know when one of his daughters passed away and let the community mourn right along with him and the family. He welcomed with open arms his mother-in-law to come stay with him and his wife and children. He printed her emancipation story for the community to be a witness to all that she had to overcome.

Jefferson was fiery, he was spicy, and he was relentless when dealing with discrimination and fighting against unjust lawmakers. He would celebrate the wins and write beautiful congratulatory pieces about Black Angeleno business owners and Black civic leaders around the nation. That support would also extend to their families. Despite Jefferson's falling out with his cofounders of the *Pasadena Searchlight* (Jefferson's first newspaper), he still dedicated space in *The Liberator* to spotlight

the daughter of his former collaborator for being the first Black graduate of Pasadena High School: "Miss [Marguerite] Prince is a worthy
and much loved young lady. Her friends and associates in Pasadena and
elsewhere are justly elated over her achievements. The Liberator extends
congratulations" (*The Liberator* June 23, 1911).

Jefferson's true pride and joy, the softness and vulnerability that shone
through in the paper, almost always related to his family. When I went
to visit the Santa Monica Woodland Hill Cemetery back in 2018, to see
how Jefferson and the family arranged their burials, I was surprised to
find that his tombstone said nothing about his political life, no reference
to his warrior-style bravery. It simply reads: "Jefferson Lewis Edmonds,
Father." Perhaps, despite his long commitment to the advancement of
Black Americans and their citizenship rights, he really only wanted to be
remembered for what was most important to him.

While he spent so much time focusing on the next generation, he
never seemed to forget the elders and those who created the inroads
for his powerful life. In the November 1910 edition of *The Liberator*,
Jefferson wrote my great-great-great-grandmother's emancipation story.
I wonder if he knew she needed her story to have a witness. Perhaps after
all the life she had lived with no real control of her comings and goings,
her trek out west and this narrative would be one she could say belonged
to her and her alone.

I'm sharing her story here because I think it represents one of Jefferson's many spiritual offerings. He knew how to celebrate his family. He
loved showing the world just how much they had overcome and all the
steps they were taking forward.

> After a life of 80 years in the South, in which she was twice sold as a slave,
> separated in childhood from her mother, and herself brought up a fam-
> ily of 11 children, Mrs. Sally Moore has arrived here from Valdosta, Ga.,
> to pass her remaining days with her son-in-law and daughter, Mr. and
> Mrs. J. L. Edmonds at Fourteenth Street and Minnesota Avenue.
>
> She made the journey alone. Though she had never been in the West
> before, Mrs. Moore says that she knew at once when she had reached the
> section of the country which is given that general designation, solely by
> the difference in the way she was treated on the train. Until she arrived

at Kansas City, she says she could not buy meals in the railroad eating houses, had only a few mouthfuls of light lunch to eat and received no assistance from anyone on the train. At Kansas City a kind hearted California woman saw her plight and aided her by procuring the lunches for her.

Mrs. Moore was born in Charles City, Va. When a young girl, her owner, S. Christian, came to California to live and she was sold on the auction block to satisfy debts and because he was afraid she might be freed on the way if sent to California. Her buyer paid $1050 for her and took her to Macon, leaving her mother behind. They never saw each other again but kept up a correspondence till the death of the older woman.

A few years later she was sold again for the same price, Henry Moore of Valdosta being the buyer. He was killed in the war. Mrs. Moore has served three generations of white folks as a cook. The years have given her few gray hairs, her eyesight is excellent and she is happy to be reunited to her daughter, from whom she had been separated for many years. Only one daughter and one son remain of the three boys and eight girls that she brought into the world.

With Jefferson's help, my great-great-great-grandmother made the journey out west in the last chapters of her life. My heart tells me that she did this knowing that despite the endless grief and woes in her Southern upbringing, that uprooting her life and enduring a long train ride westbound to enjoy a little sun, family, and rest would be what she had been searching for her whole life.

THE LIBERATOR

WO

J. L. EDMONDS

Editor J. L. Edmonds, through the columns of his paper *The Liberator*, has caused the Negro voter to decide two of the greatest political questions recently put before the voters of California.

When the question was before the people whether the women of this state should be allowed to vote, he took up their cause and made the fight that they should have the ballot, and the count of the votes on that question in the Negro precincts, these being the ones in which this paper is most read and in whose interests it is published showed that they went 2 to 1 in favor of the amendment for woman's suffrage.

For the majority in those precincts in favor of the amendment were 000 votes.

In the Presidential campaign just closed, Mr. Edmonds supported the ticket headed by Woodrow Wilson, and his experience brought on by more than sixteen years in the Democratic party based upon the belief that it was the best way to help the Negroes' civil, political and economic interests, he made a fearless fight on the machine of this State for its unmanly treatment of the Negro voters, and so great was his fight in it that the result shown in the heavy voting Negro precincts which gave more than 40 per cent. of its vote to Wilson.

The effect of his work can be better understood when a comparison of the votes of these same precincts at the last Gubernatorial or Presidential election, on both the former occasions the Democratic vote was five per cent. in the last election the vote for the Democratic ticket in the same precincts was forty three per cent. In precinct 232 which contains not a white vote, and which has 200 registered voters, but one Democratic vote was cast in the last gubernatorial election. In this same precinct Wilson received 80 votes.

NEGROES BUILDING BUSINESS BLOCKS

Until a short time ago the enterprising colored citizens of this city have devoted their attention to purchasing lots upon which elegant modern residences were built. This have been carried on so persistently for the past 15 years that the colored citizens of this City are the best housed of any similar city in the United States.

Now that the colored men have commenced the erection of business blocks a new epoch is being made which means that the Negro here is settling down to business. Following the erection by Mr. R. C. Owens of a splendid business block on Fourth Street near Central Avenue, Mr. Dan H. Adams, a well known and popular hotel man, is just completing a small but neat block at 845 East 9th Street, which will soon be occupied as a first class ice cream parlor and delicatessen. Mr. Adams has already had many calls from persons desiring to secure long lease on the property, but has decided to conduct the place himself, thus securing first class accommodations for all classes of patrons.

MR. O. E. BROOKINS WILL BUILD

Mr. O. E. Brookins, for many years custodian of the Germain Building, and who in the meantime invested his earnings in real estate, will erect immediately a $40,000 business block. With his present real estate holdings Mr. Brookins is amply able to successfully carry his new enterprise to completion. This new departure on the part of the colored men is a movement in the right direction and means that they have decided to make use of their idle capital, which has been used for years by other men in promoting enterprises that passed the word down that Negroes were not wanted. There is a large and ever increasing number of business and professional men who are suffering for permanent locations which should be

Figure 4.1 Jefferson Lewis Edmonds, early 1900s. Courtesy of The J.L. Edmonds Project.

Figure 4.2 Virginia Edmonds with family and friends at Bruce's Beach, Manhattan Beach, California, 1919. Courtesy of The J.L. Edmonds Project.

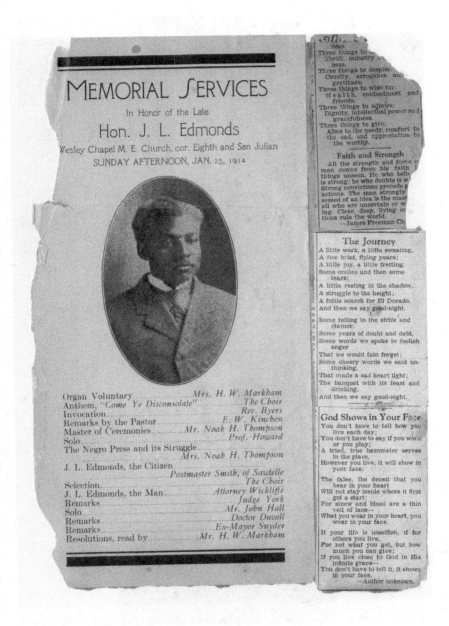

Figure 4.3 Jefferson Lewis Edmonds Obituary Funeral Program, January 1914. Courtesy of The J.L. Edmonds Project.

Figure 4.4 Edmonds Family Dinner, Sawtell, California, 1910s. Courtesy of The J.L. Edmonds Project.

Figure 4.5 Susie Edmonds, Jefferson Lewis Edmonds' Daughter, 1910s. Courtesy of The J.L. Edmonds Project.

Figure 4.6 Virginia Edmonds on the Edmonds Family Farm in Sawtell, Los Angeles, CA, 1911. Courtesy of The J.L. Edmonds Project.

Figure 4.7 Edmonds Family Farm in Sawtell, Los Angeles, CA, 1911.
Courtesy of The J.L. Edmonds Project.

Figure 4.8 Cover page of *The Liberator*, August 1902, highlighting Susie Edmonds, Jefferson's daughter who served as Assistant Editor of *The Liberator*. Courtesy of the Edmonds Family Liberator Collection with the Los Angeles Public Library. Digitized by California Revealed.

Figure 4.9 Walter Chase Edmonds, Jefferson Lewis Edmonds' grandson, 1924. Courtesy of The J.L. Edmonds Project.

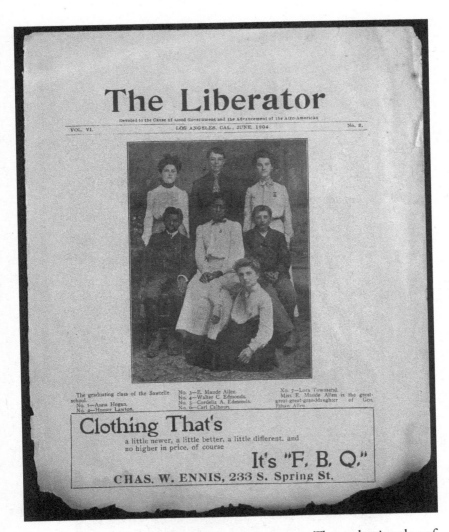

Figure 4.10 Cover page of *The Liberator*, June 1904. The graduating class of the Sawtell School, featuring Jefferson's daughter, Cordelia Edmonds, and son, Walter Chase Edmonds. Courtesy of the Edmonds Family Liberator Collection with the Los Angeles Public Library. Digitized by California Revealed.

Figure 4.11 Blanchard Edmonds, Jefferson Lewis
Edmonds' son, 1911. Courtesy of The J.L. Edmonds
Project.

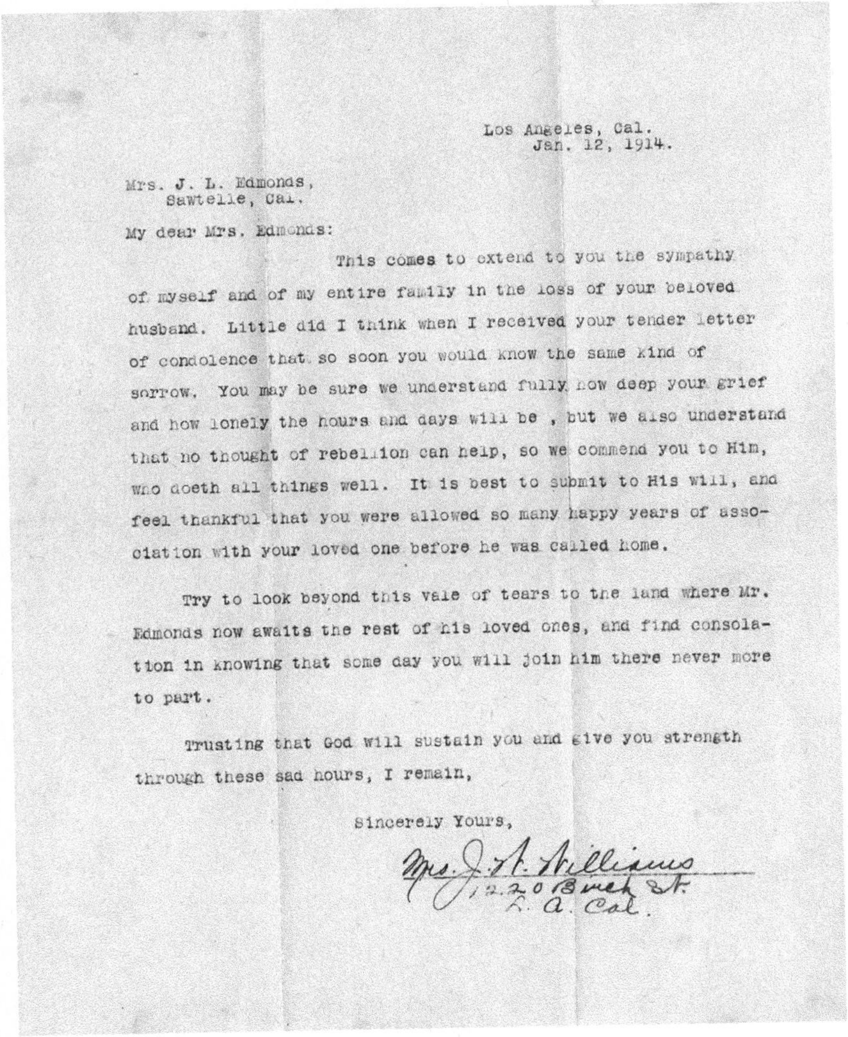

Los Angeles, Cal.
Jan. 12, 1914.

Mrs. J. L. Edmonds,
    Sawtelle, Cal.
My dear Mrs. Edmonds:

                This comes to extend to you the sympathy
of myself and of my entire family in the loss of your beloved
husband. Little did I think when I received your tender letter
of condolence that so soon you would know the same kind of
sorrow. You may be sure we understand fully how deep your grief
and how lonely the hours and days will be , but we also understand
that no thought of rebellion can help, so we commend you to Him,
who doeth all things well. It is best to submit to His will, and
feel thankful that you were allowed so many happy years of association with your loved one before he was called home.

                Try to look beyond this vale of tears to the land where Mr.
Edmonds now awaits the rest of his loved ones, and find consola-
tion in knowing that some day you will join him there never more
to part.

                Trusting that God will sustain you and give you strength
through these sad hours, I remain,

                        Sincerely Yours,

                        Mrs. J. A. Williams
                        1220 Birch St.
                        L. A. Cal.

Figure 4.12 Letter of Condolence to Mrs. J.L. Edmonds, January 1914.
Courtesy of The J.L. Edmonds Project.

Figure 4.13 Evelyn Osborne, Jefferson Lewis Edmonds'
Granddaughter, 1946. Courtesy of The J.L. Edmonds Project.

Figure 4.14 Jefferson Lewis Edmonds' Son, Jefferson Lewis Edmonds Jr., 1911. Courtesy of The J.L. Edmonds Project.

Figure 4.15 Virginia Edmonds, Jefferson Lewis Edmonds'
Daughter-in-Law, 1911. Courtesy of The J.L. Edmonds
Project.

Figure 4.16 Walter Chase Edmonds Sr. and Virginia Edmonds, 1910. Courtesy of The J.L. Edmonds Project.

CHAPTER 5

Building, Reflecting, and Future-Casting

The Liberator strongly encouraged Black Southerners to live and enjoy their lives near the ocean with the fragrance of orange blossoms in the air. Jefferson had the insight to address the foundational needs of the emerging Black Angeleno community. These families needed refuge, they needed sanctuary, they needed rest from the years of servitude and bondage. Jefferson and his contemporaries honored the newly migrated families who desired to come together for fellowship and a place to grow their Black American pride, to feel seen, to be cared for and supported.

Jefferson did this by making it clear that his newspaper was not a voice for all. He was clear that his paper was intended to prepare Black American citizens for upward mobility and transformation. "The Black press was never intended to be objective, because it didn't see the white press being objective. It often took a position; it had an attitude. This was a press of advocacy. There was news, but the news had an admitted and a deliberate slant" (Nelson 1999). However, Jefferson didn't rely solely on the newspaper as a mouthpiece for the movement toward fair citizenship for Black Americans. His promises needed to be activated within the community, with partners, and, most importantly, with the church.

Charlotta Bass, one of the infamous *California Eagle* editors, boldly wrote in her 1960 memoir *Forty Years*, "The press and the pulpit are the two main centers for the development of community consciousness."

She went on to say, "In spite of seeming differences, a high degree of solidarity, a high degree of unity along certain basic lines, developed in Los Angeles as a result of the interaction of these two forces." Much like the Black church, the Black press at the turn of the twentieth century was an institution. An institution that formed communities and defined Black leadership away from the scrutiny of white America. *The Liberator*, much like the *California Eagle*, *The Afro*, and the *Chicago Defender*, used its pages to project into the future and report on the development of Black America's pathway toward a fulfilled Black American life.

Black newspapers at the turn of the twentieth century were not just used to inform and present objective stories; they were used to incite a social revolution, to create a new Black American standard, and instill a civic responsibility. These new Black American constitutional rights were not just a gift that these formerly enslaved peoples were lucky to have but a right, and a promise that could and should be defended when violated. *The Liberator* would document notes from various social group meetings, important visits from Black thought leaders around the country, future-focused policy stances around women's rights, and much more (Bunch 2001). Jefferson, hand-in-hand with his social-justice-warrior contemporaries, co-created roadmaps and community systems that would help guide Black Angelenos on all the ways they would need to guard themselves against a return to their enslaved past. Thus was birthed the LA Forum.

The LA Forum

The Los Angeles Forum (commonly referred to as the LA Forum) was established in 1903 by Jefferson L. Edmonds; the Reverend Jarrett E. Edwards, pastor of the First AME Church; and John Wesley Coleman, a businessman (Jefferson et al. 2018). The cofounders combined Coleman's expertise in the private sector and commerce, Jefferson's knowledge of media and civic and political engagement, and Edwards's spiritual, social, and community organizing. It made for a rich and

rounded experience for new and existing Angelenos. Over the years the
LA Forum hosted debates, speeches, and town hall meetings that would
support Black Angelenos in processing the issues of the day and preparing for their tomorrows: "Any man or woman of good character is
eligible to membership and no fees are charged" (Troy 1909). Community members met weekly, first at the First AME Church and then at the
Odd Fellows' Hall at Seventh and Wall Streets.

The LA Forum is most known for philanthropic causes like raising
money for victims of the San Francisco earthquake and fire of 1906, the
building of the 28th Street YMCA, and rallying against the screening of
the film *The Birth of a Nation* in 1915. However, we find in the debates
and town halls how *The Liberator* and the work of the LA Forum helped
shape political consciousness years and sometimes decades before local
and national policy would take shape (Jefferson et al. 2018).

We see this best described through a debate over women's rights:

> The debate on Women's Suffrage last Sunday attracted a big crowd to the
> Forum. Attorney W. R. Taylor opened the debate against it in a speech
> of over an hour in length. He covered much ground. His speech being
> listened to with close attention and from the vigor and frequency of the
> applause it seemed that all male anti's had turned out. His speech was
> marked by eloquence and brilliancy but much of its effect was lost by its
> length. If he had boiled his speech down to 30 minutes it would have been
> more difficult for his opponents. In order that Attorney Simons, (white)
> of Pasadena might have a chance to reply, the time had to be extended 30
> minutes. Mr. Simons, who represented the Equal Rights League made
> splendid use of his time and answered Mr. Taylor with an argument that
> swept everything before it and women's suffrage won another victory.
>
> (*The Liberator* June 16, 1911)

It's important to note that these discussions were happening nearly
a decade before the passing of the 19th Amendment of 1920, which
granted American women the right to vote. However, many state laws
created barriers for Black Americans to get to the polls due to literacy exams and poll taxes. "While we celebrate the 19th Amendment
we should also celebrate the 1965 Voting Rights Act that made the
amendment a reality for millions of black women," Rutgers professor

Deborah Gray White and Marisa Fuentes share in reference to their 2016 book *Scarlet and Black: Slavery and Dispossession in Rutgers History.*

The work of the LA Forum helped champion and introduce the notion of Black women voters nearly forty years before any federal law was enforced. Jefferson took a very hard stance against those who opposed women's voting rights. He had this to share in a July 23, 1911, issue of *The Liberator*: "One of the most discouraging features of willful waste of valuable time is that men, members of the Forum will applaud those who attack even the good names of their own wives and mothers."

The LA Forum also explored the topics of the Back to Africa movement, a popular subject often raised in their Sunday meetings by missionaries returning from the continent. In the later years of the paper we see discussion of Back to Africa in conjunction with Black Americans migrating and settling in Liberia and Marcus Garvey's burgeoning Universal Negro Improvement Association (UNIA) movement, which encouraged those in the African diaspora to work and trade goods as one.

> The debate: Resolved that the Back to Africa movement is best for the Negro, which was to take place between Mr. Lacy and Miss M. E. Brown was postponed. Mr. Lacy pled unreadiness. He saw Miss Brown annihilate a famous young orator a few Sundays ago at the Forum and wanted time to prevent meeting a similar fate.
> (*The Liberator* April 28, 1911)

The Liberator jumps into the middle of the action of a debate that took place at a Sunday meeting. A group of young men tackled issues of labor law violations taking place in Chicago:

> The crowd at the Forum last Sunday was one of the largest in its history. The absorbing topic being the labor situation. *The Liberator*'s editorial showing the perfidy with which the colored cooks and waiters of Chicago, were treated by the white unions of that place, furnished the main topic of discussion for the evening. The addresses were able and instructive and were listened to by the vast audience with the closest attention. The ladies turned out in great numbers and showed the same interest in the absorbing topic as did the men. The addresses were remarkable for the thought brought out. Very noteworthy speeches were delivered by Rev. J. A. Stout, Messrs. S. B. Tillman, Morgan T. White and G. Walter Snell.

On the whole the speeches of the gentlemen named were far above the average.

(The Liberator April 28, 1911)

The LA Forum was clearly ahead of its time. It championed civic and social issues that would help Black Angelenos better situate themselves in the tapestry of American life. But it also created community, a place of belonging, and a roadmap for their future.

Memorable Visits

In collaboration with the LA Forum, *The Liberator* covered the California visit of W. E. B. Du Bois, then the nation's leading African American writer and thinker. While touring the state to boost participation in the National Association for the Advancement of Colored People (NAACP), Du Bois championed Los Angeles as a place with no limits on opportunities and possibilities for Black Americans. *The Liberator* worked tirelessly for months to promote this grand visit. Jefferson wanted his readers to know that Los Angeles would soon be a place for Black political power and thought leadership, and a place where dreams could be fulfilled.

In May 1913, Du Bois visited California to establish NAACP chapters in the West, and *The Liberator* captured his Los Angeles speaking tour. Jefferson served as one of his guides, showcasing the splendor of Black Los Angeles. He also reported on Du Bois's speaking tour of Southern California. Jefferson was so meticulous in his reporting that he documented the ten-car motorcade that greeted the arrival of Dr. Du Bois at the Santa Fe train station.

> Reception Committee:
> **Dr. Du Bois** was met at the Santa Fe Station on his arrival by ten automobiles, all owned by our colored business and professional men. The procession moved from the Santa Fe Station to the Y. M. C. A. in the following order:

Miss Brown Lays Out a Walking Delegate   Page 5

THE LIBERATOR

A Weekly Newspaper Devoted to the Cause of Good Government and the Advancement of the Afro-Americans.

Vol. IX   5 cts. a copy   LOS ANGELES, CAL., APRIL, 14, 1911 $1.50 a year   No. 9

"DR. W. E. B. DU BOIS"

Dr. W. E. B. Du Bois will be one of the representatives of the United States to the Universal Race Congress at London, England, next July.

Dr. Du Bois is one of the most eminent scholars in this country. His contributions to the leading publications of the country are such that they create a surprise when his racial identity becomes known, which usually brings out the exclamation—"I did not know he was colored."

Prejudice Let Loose

The attitude of certain Southern newspapers in the recent Booker Washington affair is contemptible. They seemed to take particular delight in putting the worst possible construction upon every phase of the incident that seemed to be damaging to Mr. Washington. The high character of the man, the splendid services rendered by him in behalf of his race, the contributions he has made in every part of the country toward a better relation between the white people and the Negro—all that the man stands for was ignored and hurled aside, and the latent, lurking prejudice against the Negro came at once to the surface and once more asserted itself in tones of bitter hatred.

Then, when the explanations were made, and the plain, honest

Dr. W. E. B. Du Bois

facts came out, completely clearing Mr. Washington of blame, as everybody who was free from prejudice and evil-wishing knew they would, these papers did not have the manliness to retract their miserable aspersions. They did nothing to repair the damage they had made to the reputation of a worthy man and upright citizen. Would they have treated a white man of the same high standing,

wide reputation, and recognized helpful service in the same way? Never. They would not have dared to.

But good often comes out of trouble. Mr. Washington did not lack friends in his trying distress. They believed in him. And their unshaken confidence in him cheered his soul. Among these is the President of the United States, who sent him this letter:

"I am greatly distressed at your misfortune and I hasten to write you of my sympathy, my hope that you will soon recover from the wounds inflicted by insane suspicion or viciousness, and of my confidence in you, in your integrity and morality of character, and in your highest usefulness to your race and to all the people of this country.

"It would be a nation's loss if this untoward incident in any way impaired your great power for good in the solution of one of the most difficult problems before us.

"I want you to know that your friends are standing by you in every trial, and that I am proud to subscribe myself as one."

What Mr. Taft did for Mr. Washington in that letter was more by far in his favor than all that his traducers could do in with prejudice against him, his base efforts to fill the land work and his race.—The Epworth Herald.

Figure 5.1 Cover page of *The Liberator*, April 14, 1911. *The Liberator* often included updates about W.E.B Du Bois' career and travel plans. Courtesy of the Edmonds Family Liberator Collection with the Los Angeles Public Library. Digitized by California Revealed.

(Car No. 1):—Eugene Walker, Mrs. Eugene Walker, Dr. J. A. Somerville, Dr. Du Bois.

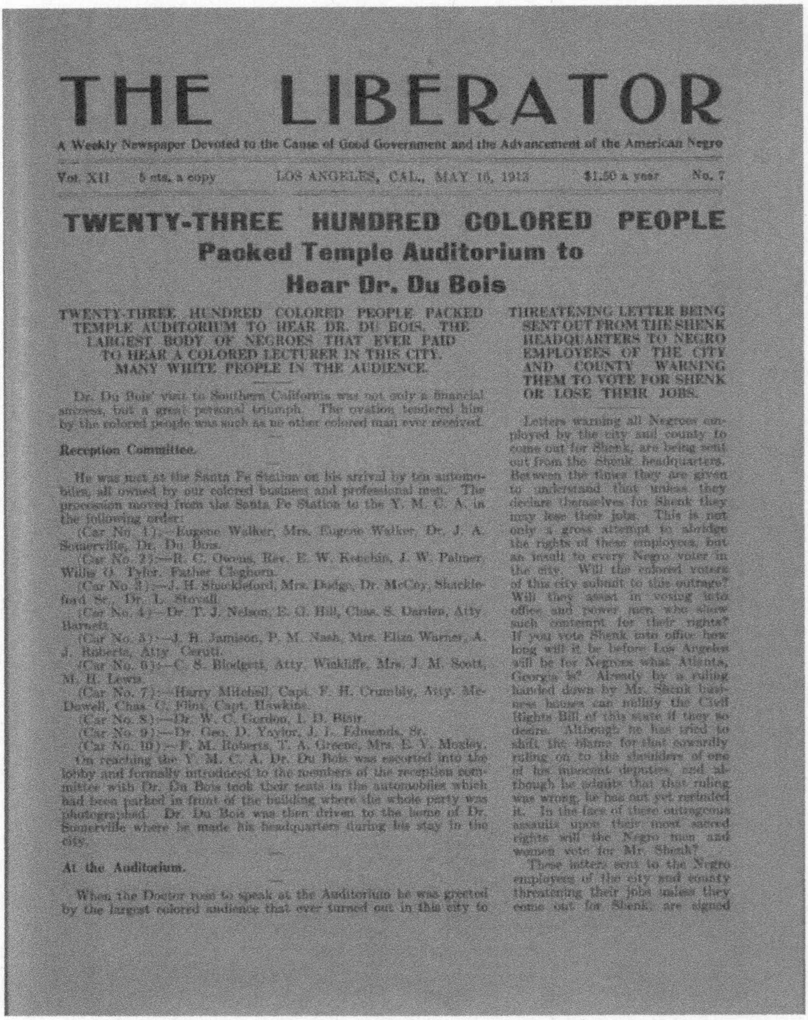

Figure 5.2 Cover page of *The Liberator*, May 16, 1913. Courtesy of the Edmonds Family Liberator Collection with the Los Angeles Public Library. Digitized by California Revealed.

(Car No. 2):—R. C. Owens, Rev. E. W. Kenchin, J. W. Palmer, Willis O. Tyler. Father Cleghorn.

(Car No. 3):—J. H. Shackleford, Mrs. Dodge, Dr. McCoy, Shackle ford Sr., Dr. L. Stovall.

(Car No. 4)—Dr. T. J. Nelson, E. G. Hill, Chas. S. Darden, Atty. Barnett.

(Car No. 5):—J. H. Jamison, P. M. Nash, Mrs. Eliza Warner, A. J. Roberts, Atty. Ceruti.

(Car No. 6):—C. S. Blodgett, Atty. Wickliffe, Mrs. J. M. Scott, M. H. Lewis.

(Car No. 7):—Harry Mitchell, Capt. F. H. Crumbly, Atty. Mc Dowell, Chas. C. Flint, Capt. Hawkins.

(Car No. 8):—Dr. W. C. Gordon, I. D. Blair.

(Car No. 9):—Dr. Geo. D. Yaylor, J. L. Edmonds, Sr.

(Car No. 10):—F, M. Roberts, T. A. Greene, Mrs. E. V. Moxley.

According to Jefferson, Du Bois was escorted into the lobby and formally introduced to the members of the reception committee. He then posed for photographs in the caravan of automobiles that were parked in front of the building.

When I read this detailed report, I immediately thought about my grandfather and the dark forest green and white courier-font label machine he used to document all his important paperwork, tapes, and records around the house. It's in the details. It runs in the blood. Just as my grandfather wanted us to remember his items far beyond his last days, so would Jefferson make sure that the Black cultural architects of the day were recognized and honored. The front page of the May 16, 1913, issue of *The Liberator* opens with the bold headline "Twenty-Three hundred colored people packed the Temple Auditorium to hear Dr. Du Bois. The largest body of Negros that ever paid to hear a colored lecture in the city." Jefferson goes on to describe Du Bois's style and eloquence as a public speaker:

> Aside from Dr. Du Bois' wide knowledge of men; his wonderful historical research, his profound reasoning, and his complete mastery of English; his ease and grace on the stage, gives him control over his audience whether composed of men from the college or the plow that few men possess. His graceful movements as he took his place on the rostrum, the smooth flow of his language, the simplicity of his words, his cold logic unaccompanied by gestures charmed and enlightened his audience beyond measure.

Figure 5.3 Colored Los Angeles greets *The Crisis* in motor cars. *The Crisis*, Vol. 6, No. 4, August 1913. Collection of the Smithsonian National Museum of African American History and Culture.

As Du Bois would share in the August 1913 California issue of the NAACP's magazine *The Crisis*, "One never forgets Los Angeles and Pasadena: the sensuous beauty of roses and orange blossoms, the air and the sunlight and the hospitality of all its races lingers long." He goes on to explain that "the colored population of Los Angeles has grown fast. It was but 2,000 in 1900, while in 1910 it was 7,500, and it has grown very rapidly since that. These colored people are pushing and energetic. They are without doubt the most beautifully housed group of colored people in the United States. They are full of push and energy and are used to working together."

This vote of approval from one of the nation's leading Black American thinkers was just the boost Jefferson and his collaborators needed to encourage new residents to relocate to the City of Angels. Printing these praise reports was an equivalent to a modern-day testimonial info ad: *Don't take my word for it, look at what our leaders have to say.* This

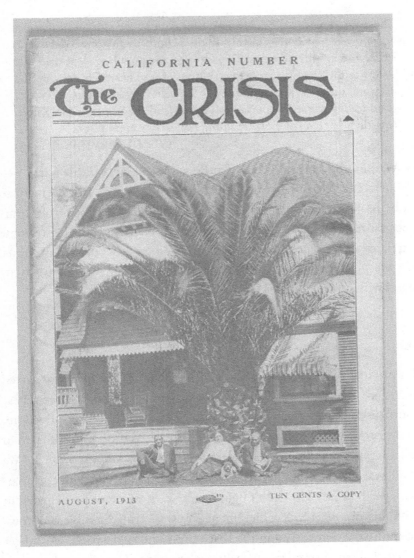

Figure 5.4 Cover of *The Crisis*, Vol. 6, No. 4, August 1913. Collection of the Smithsonian National Museum of African American History and Culture.

was also exemplified by Booker T. Washington's visit to Los Angeles in January of 1903. *The Liberator* welcomed the Tuskegee founder with great enthusiasm:

The ovation tendered Booker T. Washington by the citizens of this city was unprecedented in its history. In their efforts to do honor to the great leader and apostle of industrial education the populace went mad. No visitor to this city ever aroused an enthusiasm so heart-felt, so wide and deep and universal as that aroused by Booker T. Washington. A wave of good feeling seemed to pervade all the air and the hearts of the people, regardless of race, color or condition, beat in love and unison.

(The Liberator January 1903)

Washington, much like Dr. Du Bois, spoke highly of his warm welcome to Los Angeles and his hope for the burgeoning Black American hub. As he stated, "I want to express from the bottom of my heart the gratitude which I feel and experience this moment for the welcome extended since I set my foot on California soil. So general, so continuous, has the welcome been that I have had scarcely a moment to write to my good wife" (*The Liberator* January 1903)

Reflection

Like so many other Black publications at the time, *The Liberator* carved out space in its pages to let Black American imagination run free. These journalistic pulpits were windows into a new world of love, freedom, and exercised civic rights. As veteran journalist Vernon Jarrett shared in his interview for the film *The Black Press: Soldiers without Swords*, "We didn't exist in the other papers. We were neither born, we didn't get married, we didn't die, we didn't fight in any wars, we never participated in anything of a scientific achievement. We were truly invisible unless we committed a crime. And in the Black press, the negro press, we did get married. They showed us our babies when born. They showed us graduating. They showed our PhDs" (Nelson 1999). *The Liberator* made a quiet promise to its readers that reflections of their lives would be loved, respected, honored, and reflected back:

I am a dark brown skinned colored girl, 22 years old, of good character, have a common school education and own a little property. I would like to correspond with a young western man of the same complexion, 24 to 27 years of age and possessing all of the qualifications above mentioned.

Figure 5.5 Cover page of *The Liberator*, December 1902. Courtesy of the
Edmonds Family Liberator Collection with the Los Angeles Public Library.
Digitized by California Revealed.

Must weigh 160 pounds. All drunkards, barred. I am living in Colorado,
but all letters addressed to Miss Pattie Belle, care of The Liberator, 210
Thorpe Building, Los Angeles, Cal., will be forwarded to me without
examination.

(The Liberator April 26, 1912)

It's the "without examination" part of this personal ad that feels so loving and intimate. What a beautiful reminder that even a radical public race paper in 1904 that reached the entire nation and parts of Europe (according to Jefferson) would still run an ad to help a lonely heart twenty-two-year-old find her mate. Naturally, the advancement of the Black Angeleno community couldn't truly propel forward without addressing the internal battle of self-worth and pride.

Black Pride

Excerpt from "An Ode to Ethiopia":

> Be proud, my race, in mind and soul;
> Thy name is writ on Glory's scroll
> In characters of fire.
> High 'mid the clouds of Fame's bright sky
> Thy banner's blazoned folds now fly,
> And truth shall lift them higher.

—Paul Laurence Dunbar

Dunbar No More

On February 1906, *The Liberator* declared that "Paul Laurence Dunbar, the great negro poet, is dead. He has joined the colony of immortals on heaven's eternal camping ground and for all coming time his songs, by dispelling care, will sweeten the lives of struggling men and women."

> Earth bids farewell to all that is mortal of Dunbar, but the sweetness of his soul in the songs he has sung will ever live to bless the children of men. A race that in spite of innumerable handicaps produced, Toussaint L'Ouverture, the founder of a state, Bishop Allen the founder of a church. Frederick Douglass, the founder of Negro citizenship, Paul Laurence Dunbar the immortal singer and Tanner the world-renowned painter need have no fears for the future. (February 1906)

The Uncrowned Queen

In the June 1902 edition of *The Liberator*, Jefferson published a beautiful piece written by W. H. Council originally printed in the Black-owned San Francisco–based newspaper, *Pacific Coast Appeal*.

The Negro woman is indeed an uncrowned queen in adversity, and lifts her head as far above abuse, slander and insult as the lofty mountains kissed by the pure airs of heaven, tower above the swamps and marshes which lie at their base.

Our female element, under mother influence, attends school and church, eschews the brothels, stays at home and works, and, to our shame, is the backbone one of the Negro race today. Were it not for the Negro woman, the outlook would be dark. I am aware of the breadth of my speech when I say that the world has never furnished a higher womanhood under like conditions than the Negro woman of the South. With strong appetites and passions, penniless, often houseless, practically left to shift alone, amid debasing influences in the race and out, exposed everywhere, stumbling, falling, rising, fleeing—she goes on, washing, cooking, plowing, sowing, reaping—educating her children, building the cottage, erecting churches and schools—often supporting husband and son—this black woman deserves the admiration of the whole world.

(Council 1902)

CHAPTER 6

The Harvest

The Psychological Shift of the Black Community

Jefferson worked fervently toward building some of the foundational elements of a solid civic life: things like pride in oneself, creating a thriving community to rely on when times get hard, and a strong faith base to guide daily practices. He did this knowing that the decision to uproot and migrate from the South to Los Angeles was not solely related to securing better opportunities. In many ways, Black families that headed to the Midwest or to the East Coast did so for survival, fleeing domestic terrorism. It made them essentially refugees, rather than just pioneers or urban explorers. While the Bureau for the Relief of Freedmen and Refugees initiative administered during the Reconstruction era was meant to help with the transition for Black Americans in the South, many had to rely on each other to start afresh. Strategies, community organizations, church groups, and of course papers like *The Liberator* would serve as the true building blocks for Black Americans in their transition after slavery.

Jefferson knew that those in the early Black Angeleno community were either formerly enslaved themselves or just one generation away from slavery. The concept of freedom, mental liberation, self-actualization, and civil rights were newer concepts for this growing community. While many early Black Angelenos came to California with a trade like farming or teaching, not all were educated or literate.

Bearing this in mind, Jefferson and his cofounders of the LA Forum would read national newspapers at the community meetings so everyone was on the same page—literally. Jefferson saw the value in creating opportunities for Black Angelenos to elevate, transform, and be the masters of their own destiny. He saw being politically aware and civically informed as one of the gateways to a more fulfilled, joyous life.

Jefferson didn't just approach civil rights from one angle; he was egalitarian. He would become known for championing humanitarian rights domestically and abroad: among these, women's suffrage issues and the right to citizenship for all Black Americans. Jefferson created literary worlds and dynamic civic discourse for his readership, helping them to ground themselves in their own citizenship rights by teaching them the value in advocating and championing for others as well. "The freedom of no community is secure that grants privilege to one class that are denied to others" (*The Liberator* October 6, 1911). He guided his readers to a new way of operating, one that included worldly matters, culture, business, land ownership, expansion, and a new view of oneself and one's future as something to be proud of.

Figure 6.1 Various prominent Black Angeleno businesses featured in the January/February 1904 special edition of *The Liberator*. This business profile mirrors the profiles Jefferson helped curate in the February 12, 1909, *Los Angeles Daily Times* article commemorating President Lincoln's centennial birthday.

As *The Liberator* declared on January 3, 1913,

> It is time the Negro ceased teaching his children that they are inferior to other people merely on account of their color. Let the Negro use his noble black mother as his ideal of womanhood, remembering when he bows at the shrine of her virtue and comeliness, that he is not the only man that has worshipped at that shrine. Let his ideals for manhood, statesmanship, scholarly attainments and patriotism be his L'Ouverture's, Douglasses, Booker Washingtons, Du Boises, Dunbars and Kelly Millers.

Women's Rights Movement

The Liberator was a strong supporter of women in business and the Black women's suffrage movement. Jefferson employed his daughters as secretary and assistant editor at various times throughout *The Liberator*'s run and fought for them to have a say and voice in their positions. It was his belief that

> the woman to whom we have entrusted the care of our children is as good as we are, and the ballot will be as safe with her as it is with us. The power to write this editorial was given us by the noble women who left their homes and formed abolition societies which created the sentiment that liberated four million slaves of whom we were one. We shall do everything in our power to put women on an equality with men and thus show our appreciation of what they have done to alleviate suffering and break the shackles from the souls and bodies of men.
>
> (*The Liberator* March 31, 1911)

For nearly a year leading up to the October 10, 1911 passage of the California voter rights bill, which granted voting rights to women, Jefferson printed powerful op-eds and shared recaps of the women's suffrage debate series hosted by the LA Forum. He wanted his readers to know that this ballot measure was not to be taken lightly. "The ballot is the weapon by which individuals and communities can maintain their freedom," Jefferson said, urging his readers to consider how they defined American citizenship as it related to extending those rights to others (*The Liberator* October 6, 1911).

"If the American Negro hopes to secure the full enjoyment of his rights as an American citizen, he will have to be willing to grant them to every man and woman in this country" (*The Liberator* October 6, 1911). Once the bill passed, Jefferson and his contemporaries at the LA Forum took full advantage of this new state

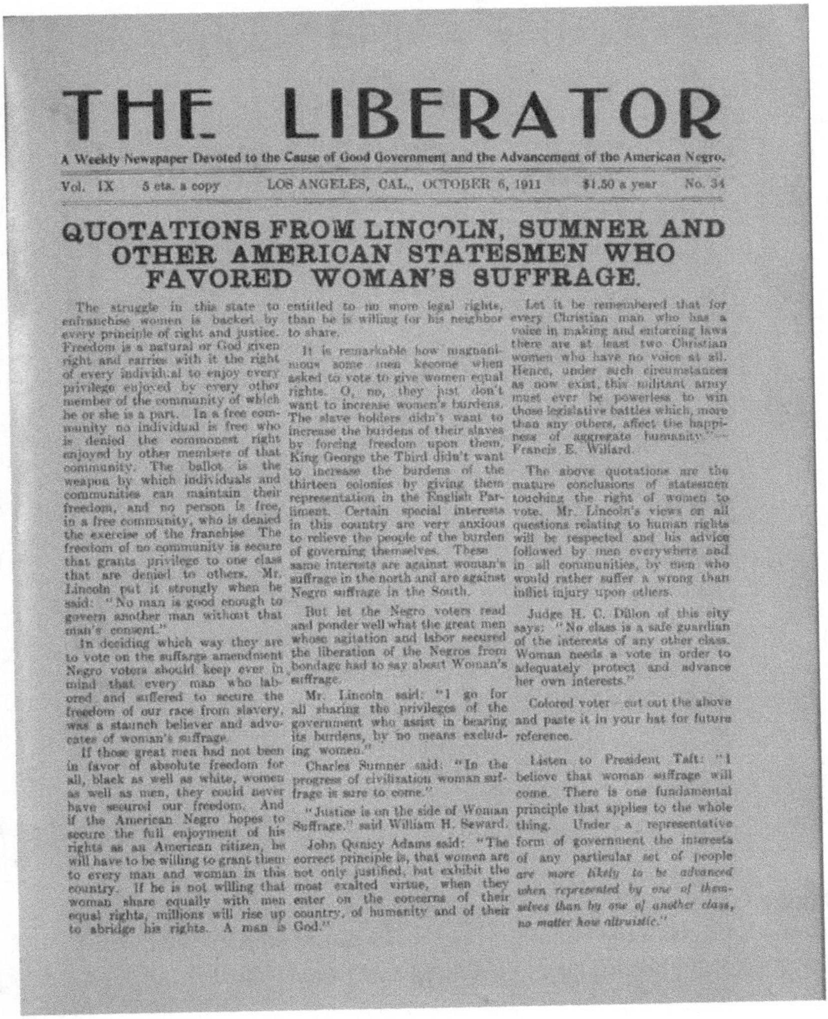

THE LIBERATOR

A Weekly Newspaper Devoted to the Cause of Good Government and the Advancement of the American Negro.

Vol. IX 5 cts. a copy LOS ANGELES, CAL., OCTOBER 6, 1911 $1.50 a year No. 34

QUOTATIONS FROM LINCOLN, SUMNER AND OTHER AMERICAN STATESMEN WHO FAVORED WOMAN'S SUFFRAGE.

The struggle in this state to enfranchise women is backed by every principle of right and justice. Freedom is a natural or God given right and carries with it the right of every individual to enjoy every privilege enjoyed by every other member of the community of which he or she is a part. In a free community no individual is free who is denied the commonest right enjoyed by other members of that community. The ballot is the weapon by which individuals and communities can maintain their freedom, and no person is free, in a free community, who is denied the exercise of the franchise. The freedom of no community is secure that grants privilege to one class that are denied to others. Mr. Lincoln put it strongly when he said: "No man is good enough to govern another man without that man's consent."

In deciding which way they are to vote on the suffarge amendment Negro voters should keep ever in mind that every man who labored and suffered to secure the freedom of our race from slavery, was a staunch believer and advocates of woman's suffrage.

If those great men had not been in favor of absolute freedom for all, black as well as white, women as well as men, they could never have secured our freedom. And if the American Negro hopes to secure the full enjoyment of his rights as an American citizen, he will have to be willing to grant them to every man and woman in this country. If he is not willing that woman share equally with men equal rights, millions will rise up to abridge his rights. A man is entitled to no more legal rights, than he is willing for his neighbor to share.

It is remarkable how magnanimous some men become when asked to vote to give women equal rights. O, no, they just don't want to increase women's burdens. The slave holders didn't want to increase the burdens of their slaves by forcing freedom upon them. King George the Third didn't want to increase the burdens of the thirteen colonies by giving them representation in the English Parliment. Certain special interests in this country are very anxious to relieve the people of the burden of governing themselves. These same interests are against woman's suffrage in the north and are against Negro suffrage in the South.

But let the Negro voters read and ponder well what the great men whose agitation and labor secured the liberation of the Negros from bondage had to say about Woman's suffrage.

Mr. Lincoln said: "I go for all sharing the privileges of the government who assist in bearing its burdens, by no means excluding women."

Charles Sumner said: "In the progress of civilization woman suffrage is sure to come."

"Justice is on the side of Woman Suffrage," said William H. Seward.

John Quincy Adams said: "The correct principle is, that women are not only justified, but exhibit the most exalted virtue, when they enter on the concerns of their country, of humanity and of their God."

Let it be remembered that for every Christian man who has a voice in making and enforcing laws there are at least two Christian women who have no voice at all. Hence, under such circumstances as now exist, this militant army must ever be powerless to win those legislative battles which, more than any others, affect the happiness of aggregate humanity."—Francis E. Willard.

The above quotations are the mature conclusions of statesmen touching the right of women to vote. Mr. Lincoln's views on all questions relating to human rights will be respected and his advice followed by men everywhere and in all communities, by men who would rather suffer a wrong than inflict injury upon others.

Judge H. C. Dillon of this city says: "No class is a safe guardian of the interests of any other class. Woman needs a vote in order to adequately protect and advance her own interests."

Colored voter cut out the above and paste it in your hat for future reference.

Listen to President Taft: "I believe that woman suffrage will come. There is one fundamental principle that applies to the whole thing. Under a representative form of government the interests of any particular set of people *are more likely to be advanced when represented by one of themselves than by one of another class, no matter how altruistic.*"

Figure 6.2 Cover of *The Liberator*, October 6, 1911. Courtesy of the Edmonds Family Liberator Collection with the Los Angeles Public Library. Digitized by California Revealed.

Figure 6.3 Vote for Women Advertisement in *The Liberator*, October 6, 1911. Courtesy of the Edmonds Family Liberator Collection with the Los Angeles Public Library. Digitized by California Revealed.

law and supported the development of women-led voter leagues, canvassing, and campaign-building. They continued to invest in public discourse around shared rights between men and women, helping to create an appetite for social change and community-wide civic engagement.

While other Black newspapers around the country, like the *Pittsburgh Courier* or the *Chicago Defender*, were focusing on issues of discrimination and the transition from slavery to newfound freedom and citizenship, *The Liberator* did all that and more. Jefferson used his paper's platform to dive into more nuanced and applied forms of citizenship. His words were beyond theory and instruction; he was of the Booker T. Washington ilk. He was inspired by Washington's Tuskegee University philosophy, which created educational pathways that conjured innovation, drew from lived experiences, and cultivated pride and power. He used those values as a template for how he and his contemporaries engaged in community-building. He knew that if you had a strong home where women felt their voice mattered, they would link arm-in-arm with Black men and start building businesses, start investing in homeownership, follow local politics, and vote on issues that inspired them. He was strategic in his approach to building a strong, lasting Black community. You can't exercise your citizenship without having a base, a community, a family to experience life with.

Land and Home Ownership

For most people, surviving slavery, enduring the Reconstruction era, securing employment, and purchasing a home would have been more than enough. Brave souls like Jefferson and his creative partner and collaborator, Noah D. Thompson, knew that securing a stable life for oneself wasn't enough. They knew that if families were willing to travel thousands of miles westward to start a new life, they would need support, they would need love, and they would need a plan.

Together, they started a real estate brokerage firm and purchased acres and acres of land to divide up into plots to sell to newly arriving Black families. They ran ads in nearly every edition of the paper encouraging readers to think beyond themselves and plan for the road ahead: "FOR SALE.—At a bargain, two vacant lots in the Furlong Home Tract. This property will make a splendid income property if improved. See Noah

D. Thompson, N. E. corner 55th and Long Beach Ave. Phone south 1651, or J. L. Edmonds, Room 210 Thorpe Bldg. Phone Main 2051" (*The Liberator* September 5, 1913).

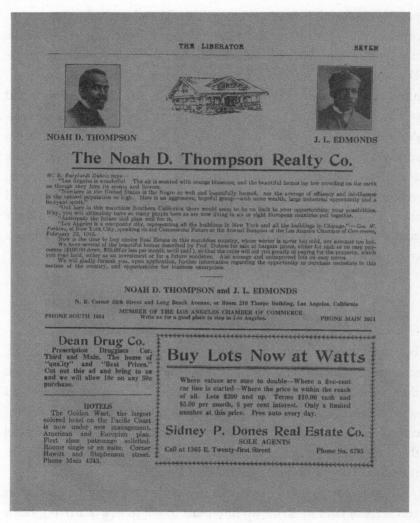

Figure 6.4 Jefferson Lewis Edmonds and Noah D. Thompson Real Estate Advertisement in *The Liberator*, August 29, 1913. Courtesy of the Edmonds Family Liberator Collection with the Los Angeles Public Library. Digitized by California Revealed.

Noah Thompson worked with Booker T. Washington at the Tuskegee Institute from 1909 to 1911 before moving to Los Angeles with his wife, Eloise A. Thompson, née Bibb. He later served as the president of the Los Angeles branch of Marcus Garvey's Universal Negro Improvement Association. Both Thompson and his wife were gifted journalists. Eloise was a talented playwright who wrote for the *Los Angeles Sunday Tribune* and later *Opportunity Magazine* (*New York Age* January 14, 1928). Noah wrote for the *Los Angeles Times*, *Evening Press*, and the *Morning Tribune* (Beasley 1919).

Thompson and Jefferson worked hand-in-hand, and Thompson took on the editorial position of the paper when Jefferson got sick toward the end of his life. You'll find Jefferson referencing how the Thompson family grocery store on Long Beach Avenue in Downtown LA would procure products from businesses who advertised in *The Liberator*. He would boast about how Thompson visited newly opening Black-owned businesses and requested meetings with the managers to help recruit Black Angeleno women looking for work. Jefferson was very transparent about how committed he was to having his fellow Black Angelenos "buy Black," invest in the Black press, and support one another.

International Viewpoints and Global Citizenship

The Liberator's decision to report on international news was one way to orient Black Angelenos in their own citizenship rights in America while also introducing them to the world of global politics. Jefferson wanted his readers to have opinions and discussions and come up with solutions to some of the changing dynamics happening abroad. His more impassioned international subjects were the Spanish—American War in the Philippines and the Liberia settlements in West Africa. *The Liberator* took a bold stance against American imperialism and fought hard to protect Black Angelenos from getting caught in the crosshairs of America's clandestine and immoral foreign affairs.

Jefferson shared this in a letter to the *Los Angeles Times* on May 30, 1902: "Today, while the colored troops are in the faraway east, fighting to protect life and property in the Philippines, the lives and property of their brethren at home are being ruthlessly destroyed. The cry of our dying, from the stake or some other method of slow death sends to heaven an almost unbroken wail." A question he posed repeatedly in his articles to the mainstream press and *The Liberator* was: How can we fight these wars and attempt to control other countries while we haven't honored constitutional rights for Black Americans domestically?

In the early years of the paper, Jefferson did extensive reporting on the Spanish—American War. Black papers around the nation held mixed positions about Black troops fighting wars for a country that often deprived Black Americans of their own rights. We see Jefferson starting with a more idealistic yet cautious view of Black troops' involvement. In a joint statement from the executive committee of the Negro National Democratic League at the Sixth Biennial session in 1900, Jefferson and his committee members asserted that "the glorious and untarnished record of the Negro soldiers, in all the wars of the country has been a source of pride to the race." Their printed statement in the July 21, 1900, edition of *Broad Ax* declared that Colonel Theodore Roosevelt wouldn't be the decorated war hero without the Black troops, "who saved the day at El Caney, San Juan Hill."

At the close of the war, the 1898 Treaty of Paris granted America control of Puerto Rico, Guam, and the Philippines for a fee of $20 million (approximately $700 million today) to Spain for their infrastructure investment (A Treaty of Peace between the United States and Spain. 1899). Jefferson was weary of the national chatter regarding citizenship and civil rights for the new territories.

Black Americans who had already seen the constitutional change of the 15th Amendment and the resistance and blockages that prevented them from exercising that right became top of mind for Jefferson in regard to the new territories. In a letter to the *Los Angeles Times* on September 13, 1907, titled "Let Those People Go," Jefferson stated that

"American rule in those distant islands has been disastrous . . . I do not favor selling the islands to Japan or any other nation. In lieu of this, a time should be set to give them independence or grant territorial rights." He goes on to say, "I was once a slave, so it can be easily imagined how horrifying to me is the idea of selling men."

It was Jefferson's belief that the islanders "will never be admitted to equal citizenship, nor their territory to statehood in this republic." Some twenty years after he was granted voting rights, he was savvy enough to know that a new constitutional change doesn't mean they will be respected or enforced. Jefferson shared his views that the Philippines would never get statehood or citizenship: "The promise of statehood is a process of sowing dragon's teeth" (*The Liberator* May 1901).

Jefferson concluded his letter to the *Times* by saying,

> When the negro is as free in Mississippi as the white man is in Massachusetts; when the white man reaches that plane of manly self-dependence that he no longer feels the need to class legislation to keep him ahead of the negro, when our "labor and trust" problems have been amicably settled, we may then be able to "benevolently assimilate" the Philippines, until then we had better let those people go.

> (*Los Angeles Times* September 13, 1907).

The Back to Africa movement taking roots in Liberia was often shared and discussed at Forum town hall meetings. *The Liberator* also reported positively on missionaries returning from different parts of West Africa and all the wonders of their voyages. However, Jefferson's stance on staying put was unwavering. He really knew how to bring the drama. He asked in an April 11, 1913, edition of *The Liberator*, after all the years of toiling in the American soil and fighting for equal rights, how could he give up and leave the country? He wanted to see the fruits of his labor. Even when a subscriber wrote in and suggested Jefferson receive the appointment of Minister of Libria, he responded with: "We would not accept the Liberian mission if it was handed to us on a platter."

In the November 1911 issue of the *The Liberator* an article titled "The Truth about Liberia" includes excerpts from the UK-based *Cornhill Magazine* written by E. D. Morel. This article narrates a very critical viewpoint of the issues happening in Liberia:

> Liberia is populated by the descendants of American negroes, who, prior to the Civil War, were sent there by the American Colonization Society; equipped with agricultural and mechanical machinery, seeds, animals, clothing, furniture, merchandise and money, with the expectation that they would gradually civilize and assimilate with the people of adjacent tribes, and build up an African republic that should demonstrate the capacity of the negro race to achieve a high degree of civilization and progress, and that they would establish a government that would command the respect and friendship of the nations of the world, and serve as a factor in solving the then existing problem of African slavery.
>
> A handful of American negroes, inflated with the exaggerated notion of their own importance which it has been the policy of the Powers to foster for their own purposes; deeply suspicious of Europeans; utterly incapable of imposing their authority upon the aboriginal population who do not acknowledge them; possessing neither administrators nor soldiers: corrupt and incompetent, play their foolish little farce of self-government, with their Cabinet, Senate, and House of Representatives; indulge in their wretched little disputes, their elections, their religious bickerings, their theological disquisition; existing at all, not by merit of their own labors . . . [it is] unfair to the Liberians themselves, gravely unjust to the aboriginal population, and a bar to all possibility of progressive advance on their part.

Jefferson was clear in his view that resettling in Liberia and practicing nation-building alongside the American government was doomed from the start. Much like his advocacy of the Filipino community, his concerns about forcing American values and policies on a nation rich with their own culture and systems would not be a fruitful endeavor.

Domestically, all Black towns like Mound Bayou in Mississippi and Allensworth in California received continual praise and support from *The Liberator*. Jefferson would often give updates on their self-governing approaches. He ran an article written by Booker T. Washington that beamed with pride as he spoke of Mound Bayou's new banking system:

"The Bank of Mound Bayou now enjoys correspondence with banks in Memphis, in Louisville, and in Vicksburg, with the National Reserve Bank of the City of New York" (Washington 1911). Jefferson boasted about hosting Lt. Col-Allensworth at his family home in Sawtelle in February 1906. Together they visited the Old Soldiers' Home, a veterans' community located in Santa Monica, and toured several real estate investments in the Sawtelle area (*The Liberator* February 1906).

Lt. Col. Allensworth retired later that year, and the Southern California Real Estate and Investment Company hosted a banquet in his honor. *The Liberator* shared how moving the speakers were and how proud they were of his achievements within the United States Army. Allensworth, along with Professor William Payne, Dr. William H. Peck, J. W. Palmer, and Harry Mitchell, founded a free Black colony that they would later name Allensworth in Tulare County (Mikell 2017). *The Liberator* documented the progress of the town development and printed ads about purchasing plots of land: "Allensworth Lands, $2 down, $2 a month" (*The Liberator* November 1910).

It's my hunch that Jefferson saw how valuable it was to showcase Black American governance and community-building on the local and national levels. This civic pride extended to how often he reported on social groups, church groups, and political organizing associations in Los Angeles. It's as if he wanted to prove to himself and his readership: *We can do this. We pay our taxes, we are industrious, we know how to be citizens. It's America that is misinformed of our greatness.*

PART III

Preparing for Our Legacy

All That Blooms

My mom and I were visiting my grandparents like we did every week. But this visit would be one that my mom will never let me forget. Sweetmama and my Grandpa John were hosting a few friends who had just returned from a Christian mission trip overseas. Dr. Taylor was the special guest. I helped prepare the cheese and crackers and tuna with Sweetmama earlier that afternoon and then ran upstairs and nestled into my favorite spot in the blue room. I knew this visit was grown folks' business, so I stayed out of the way. I sprawled out on the twin bed near the big window with my notebook, pink fluffy feather pen like the one from the movie *Clueless*, and the CD player my dad got me for Christmas the year before. My eleven-year-old self was listening intently to my new Aqua CD on repeat, dedicated, and I mean *dedicated*, to writing all the lyrics to "Barbie Girl" so that I could recite it perfectly for my friends at school.

Later that afternoon, my mom came upstairs and told me Dr. Taylor wanted to see me and pray for me. He was a slender, delicate man in a white suit with gold trimmings, Liberace-style. His face was calm and dreamy but his eyes were direct and piercing. He put his hands on my head and closed his eyes. I closed mine too. Sweetmama, my mom, and my Grandpa John all started praying and speaking in tongues. I was used to the Christian heavenly language of tongues, but it still confused me as a kid. I was silent but the spirit of the room made tears run down my cheeks. Dr. Taylor touched my face.

This is one of my mom's favorite parts of the story, so the following account is a verbal collage of my eleven-year-old memory, my mom's very adult memory, and, of course, the spirit of the exchange that took place that afternoon:

"Okay Mommy, what do you remember about that day?"

"He told us, 'God had something very special for you. He said it was something that you would share with the world. Global!" she said.

She really emphasized the "global," and opened her eyes really big. My mom talks about my dramatic storytelling but clearly it comes from somewhere.

"Did he say anything else? I remember him mentioning a puzzle and pieces of paper."

"He said it would not be revealed to you until a specific time and until the Lord calls you into this blessing. He then asked if you like to draw. He asked if you like to write poetry. You said, 'yes.' He then asked you, 'Do you like to doodle and draw on tiny pieces of paper and take notes?' You said, 'Yes.' He said keep all the papers, notebooks and scrap papers because they're going to be important for you later. When God reveals the whole story you'll know what to do with all those little pieces of paper. It will be like a puzzle. Right now, you have the pieces. God will show you what to do when the puzzle is complete. It will be then that you share this story with the world. He told us it will be a blessing to hundreds of thousands of people."

"Wow, this has a bit more meaning since I'm literally writing a book about our family's paper and all the documents, letters, and articles I've collected over the last decade."

"I know, that's why I keep reminding you of this story. You know, Dr. Taylor passed away six months after that. You met him in God's perfect timing. It was the right place and the right time, Arie!"

"Keep going."

Fast-forward to my mid-twenties, and I'm just graduating from college and living in Philadelphia. Years after my transcendent encounter with Dr. Taylor, I wasn't thinking about my scrap papers, our family news-paper, or that Aqua CD. Dreams of Jefferson would call me back to LA and interrupt my search for artistic purpose in the City of Brotherly Love. Jefferson came to me one night in a dream, wearing a three-piece black and gray suit, with three of his sons. They all stared at me lovingly and directed my attention to a grassy mountain top. It was more like a hill, nothing too overpowering or epic. They picked me up and flew me over this hill and told me it was time to come back to LA and that they would take care of everything. Jefferson told me not to worry. My Aunt Stephanie called me about a week later and told me of a similar dream, but this time it was my dad asking me to return to Los Angeles. That's when I decided to listen and head westbound.

Jefferson's promise to me was true. Within a few short months I got a car, a new apartment, new friends, and a man—look at God! I started a job right away working for a nonprofit in downtown LA. Most of the buildings I worked in during the years to follow were just a few blocks from where the ancient secret elder sycamore tree once provided its shade to arriving Angelenos. In its prime, El Aliso stood 60 feet tall and over 200 feet wide, providing wisdom, safekeeping, and community-gathering for hundreds of years.

Before I share the legacy of this powerful tree, let me first ask you to sit calmly. Reflect on the times you've been at the mercy of forces beyond you. Think about a time when you thought you were just gliding along in your life and something big and sweeping rushes in and invites you to reroute your journey. This tree, *The Liberator*, Jefferson, becoming a mother, and so many other invisible forces have been that for me. What about you?

El Aliso was a meeting place and hallowed ground, where the indigenous Tongva people would travel hundreds of miles to hold meetings under what they called the "Council Tree." In the winter of 1779, King Carlos III of Spain issued an order to his delegates in Mexico to recruit families to become the first settlers of *El Pueblo de la Reina de los Ángeles*, "The town of the Queen of the Angels" (Bass 1960, 1). By 1781, the 44 Pobladores (early settlers) of African, Indigenous, and Spanish descent migrated to present-day Los Angeles and first settled near El Aliso. This tree became a life force and a guiding post for generations of people in the City of Angels. By the mid-1800s, as business started growing around the tree, it slowly started to wither and become barren. By 1895, a lumberjack was hired to chop El Aliso down. "People came from all over the city to witness its demise and to get chips of the tree for souvenirs. The Chamber of Commerce retained a slice for display" (Wallace 2018).

In *The Hidden Life of Trees* (Wohlleben 2015), Peter Wohlleben talks about how the roots of an elder tree cut down still communicate with its neighboring trees. They act as ancestors communicating from the other side, sending messages under the forest floor alerting its tree family of danger or new weather patterns. Learning about the fascinating world of trees has helped me better understand the hidden legacies in my city, my neighborhood, and my family: that these roots are always talking. Always communicating, and remembering for us when we choose to forget.

Today, a plaque has replaced the tree on a small patch of land on the left-hand side entrance of US 110 freeway off Alameda Street. Millions of Angelenos have passed through this area and still today the area surrounding this ghost of a tree is at the epicenter for council, commerce, and connection. The now-phantom branches of our long gone dear elder tree guard us from the sun and protect the legacies of souls dating back centuries. Whether we acknowledge it or not, El Aliso is there, holding all the secrets, promises, and plans of all the powerful decisions made about our beloved City of Angels. Much like the ancient roots of El Aliso, whispering to us Angelenos that Los Angeles can still be a city of greatness, Jefferson's promises of a brighter, more powerful, and civically engaged life for Black Americans are also whispering. His stories hidden in the stacks of the Los Angeles Public Library and in the hearts of his family members scattered around LA County—we still hear the call. When we get really quiet and pay attention, we can still hear the call to ease into a life more audacious than our ancestors could have ever dreamed for us.

Adina

To My Sweet Sweet Adina Baby,

I didn't know you were coming, but I'm glad you did. All of us, not just
your dad and I, but our family, our city, this world is better because you
are here. All the puzzle pieces I've been putting together over the years, all
the stories that have been collected by your grandfathers, will be given to you.
It gets to have more meaning and weight because you've taught me that I
don't need to carry it all by myself. Thank you for joining our family and
maybe one day you'll want to record, document, and remember just like
me, your grandfather, his father, and his grandfather. We will be with
you every step of the way. You will never have to hold this legacy by yourself.
Thank you for choosing us. We'll do all we can to stand by your side as you
start facing the world. It's our prayer that you'll be equipped and prepared
to withstand anything that comes your way. You'll be ready because you will
know about all the hands who wrote new futures for you to live in. You'll
know all the hearts that dreamed up new realities for you to step into. Baby
Adina, I tell you that promises, prayers, and planning have been passed
down for centuries. Just for you. Just for you to grab a hold of and use when
you're ready to create your own vision for the world.

    You will have all the building blocks, all the support, all the tools to con-
struct something miraculous, something dazzling, something delicious and
pure. We can't wait to see what you'll do with all this history. Your dad and
I know it's going to be absolutely fabulous. We love you, Adina baby. We
love you in this lifetime and all the other times we get to do life together.

CHAPTER 7

What I Learned

When I first met my husband he would take me to funeral parties, the long two- or three-day celebrations Ghana is best known for. He would pick me up in his old-school baby blue BMW with racer stripes on the side. The Ghana flag air freshener and black beaded rosary swung back and forth as we whipped through the Accra traffic, pulling up on the shoulder lane and passing cars and trucks with ease. We'd get to his auntie's house and be invited to sit outside on white plastic folding chairs, under a big white tent, the modern-day version of a tree—and we'd wait. We'd sit for thirty minutes, an hour or two. We'd nod as various family members would flow in and out of the courtyard and we'd wait. Ghana has taught me so much about waiting. Sitting. Being.

The events go on for days. Each community gathering calls for a different color: white, black, or red, all symbolizing specific transitions, grief, mourning, and celebration. I didn't know it then, but all those funerals liberated my thinking around archiving and memory work.

I had always held on so tight to the stories from the elders in the family. I would visit churches and libraries, sometimes with only four or five guests in the room, and tell the stories of Jefferson and all the parts of his legacy I had cobbled together from notes left from my grandpa and other ancestors. I'd talk about *The Liberator* and its power. I spent so much time encouraging Black folks to preserve everything they had. I encouraged them to record interviews with their grandparents. *Make sure you save important letters, photos. Make sure, make sure, make sure,*

I'd chant. I'd preach the importance of documentation. I dedicated years to working with community members on how to preserve our memories and avoid extinction. Fear of erasure would be the motivating sentiment to my work at that time. Fear of being forgotten would fuel my purpose.

American society suffers from a very severe case of historical amnesia, and I used my preservation and archival work as a way to combat that very issue. My work became a form of resistance and activism. However, my time in Ghana taught me how to put down the shield and sword and remember, and honor the past without the grief, without the hurt, without the scarcity. Sitting at so many funeral parties watching aunties and uncles sing and dance, drink and cry, and eat and celebrate taught me about the act of remembering. So many Ghanaian families come together to celebrate their dearly departed ones a year later and many years after that. These funerals helped me approach my memory work the same way. I slowly started embracing Black archival work from a place of abundance, love, and celebration. I started looking forward, focusing on the future while keeping the past in mind. The collecting of Black stories didn't have to feel so dire. It didn't have to feel so heartbreaking.

Perhaps I was just waiting for the chance to catch my breath. I had been on a decade-long quest to find Jefferson, his life, his legacy, myself. Along the way I started encouraging other Black families to explore and connect the dots to their lineage. I felt such a deep responsibility to make these parts of history become part of our collective memory. It now gets to be a gift that I'm offering future generations. It's my love offering, and I've been collecting these stories because I love my family and because I want those who generously shared their stories with me to also feel loved, cared for, and honored in the process.

*

Back during my research phase at the start of my search for Jefferson, I would read Black papers from the 1900s just as frequently as current day news. My research hovered somewhere between the living and the dead. In this small crawlspace between both worlds, I'd set up my voice recorder on my iPhone, my journal, pen and paper, and start notating anything that caught my eye on the microfiche machines and digital archives. I'd sit. I'd listen and wait to hear what stories wanted to come forward. Akin to a medium, I let the spirits tell me who they wanted to celebrate and bring to the light first. As I navigated the libraries, special collections, and repositories around the nation, I didn't always know what I was looking for. I might have a few dates or a few names, but mostly I went there to listen.

My grandfather shared stories here and there about Jefferson and *The Liberator*, but he passed away when I was quite young. We didn't spend a lot of time looking back. Much like other Black families, we learned to detach from our painful past, in order to survive and exist. But that doesn't mean that my family didn't collect, preserve, or keep watch over our family history. Each generation played a role. Some family members collected the pictures, like my cousins Carol and Lauryl, while others held on to the periodicals, like my dad, and still others advocated for digitization and public scholarship. Take a look at this letter from my Uncle David Carlisle Sr. to Jefferson's daughters:

> April 1, 1976
> Dear Aunt Lena and Aunt Cordelia,
> I believe the positive action to take at this time is to reopen the discussion with the Microfilming Corporation of America who proposed to be of assistance in microfilming and placing copies of *The Liberator* in libraries and universities for research purposes.
> The important objective you have is to stimulate an interest in and expand the public's awareness of the many contributions your father made. Getting microfilms of *The Liberator* into prime locations where others can avail themselves of the newspaper may result in significant interest in these volumes from serious researchers—this result is exactly what you are seeking to achieve.
> Love,
> Dave

He sweetly and professionally adds: "PS: Please understand that nothing I say to you should take precedence over advice and counsel you may have already received from your lawyer in this matter."

Years later, in 2019, my dad and I partnered with the Los Angeles Public Library and the California State Library system to digitize our collection of *The Liberator.* Just like our family members (now ancestors) detailed above, we wanted to ensure that the newspaper's significance was shared and available globally for researchers, students, historians, and artists. We knew that Jefferson wouldn't have kept each paper and bound them into books if he didn't want them to be found and remembered for future generations.

*

I was able to build on the foundation of research, recordkeeping, and advocacy done by my ancestors. I also knew that not everyone has that experience in their own family. I understand that it's a sacred act when Black American elders offer an opening into their past. It's an honor to have made them feel light enough, free enough, to tell me what they've seen. What they've endured. These rare and special openings would emerge at some of my storytelling workshops that I hosted over the years at universities, cultural centers, and libraries around the nation.

I typically start the workshops by telling the audience about Jefferson's life in Mississippi, his political organizing and canvassing during the Reconstruction era. I share how he knew he could only get so far by staying in Mississippi. He knew he needed to leave. It's at this point in the story that I pause and I ask the audience to turn to their neighbor. All the Black folks in the audience are well prepared; this is a very common request in Black churches around the globe. We spend half the church service turning to our neighbors and affirming them, warning them of sin, and reminding them they are loved. For everyone else in the audience, they are in for a treat. I start by saying, "Tell your neighbor about a time when you knew you had to leave. When you knew you had to take a leap of faith."

The room becomes a whisper for just a minute or so before it gradually turns to a murmur. Then the laughter and the giggles erupt. I watch strangers embrace after their allotted time and exchange phone numbers.

About ten minutes in, I start to invite the room to recenter and join me for the next chapter of Jefferson's life. I typically ask a brave soul to share what they learned from their neighbor before moving forward. The stories that come from the elders in the room often bring me to my knees and render me speechless.

Over the years, I've heard stories of Black folks leaving the South in the 1940s after family members were lynched, others having the courage to leave violent domestic abuse situations, some starting their first business with very little support. So many guests would tell me that they had never shared their stories in public—or at all, for that matter. My attempt to bring Jefferson's legacy alive and create an embodied experience for folks learning this history for the first time became an opportunity for Black stories to be seen, to be heard, be affirmed.

At the start of my journey with collective memory work, I naively thought that it's a shame more Black American stories and histories aren't handed down generation after generation. How do we ensure that we collect all we can before it's too late?

But now, over a decade and a half later, I'm recognizing that the right stories do get passed down. Just like my family kept so many artifacts and stories, many other Black American families have done the same. We have a long history of preserving and keeping important items safe.

I'm finding that those secret stories and artifacts are just in need of a home and an advocate. They are in need of the mouthpiece, a storyteller, the journalist, the podcasters who will help Black Americans digest our past and work toward a future where we can integrate and embody our histories. I slowly realized that my work needed to create opportunities to memorialize these statures of hope, pain, grief, and erasure. Just like sitting in Ghana at the funeral parties, we just need a ritual, an opportunity to lay these stories and artifacts to rest so we can free up our time here on Earth to create something new, something grand, something never before seen.

With this shift in perspective, I started working with community groups and small businesses all over South Los Angeles and began scanning family photos and recording oral histories. I partnered with a dear friend and contemporary, Kelli Jackson, owner of Hanks Mini Market in Hyde Park, and together with my young cousins Corey, Colin, Nash, and Taylor, we started documenting our community. If our Los Angeles stories of compassion, triumph, and community togetherness didn't make it into the major news cycles, that's okay. Our aim was to make sure these stories will be collected and housed in a digital archive for future scholars, artists, students, and historians to see just how Black South Angelenos felt about themselves. My work was slowly transforming and rooting in possibility. We were not the first group of folks to go around documenting their community, and we won't be the last. Being the keeper of my own family history was just one part of my journey. This next iteration has been fertile ground for me—and I'm eager to see where this work takes me next.

CHAPTER 8

Jefferson's Legacy

Jefferson always pushed ahead. As his civil rights efforts in Mississippi were being stifled, he courageously made the decision to move to LA and create a new reality for himself and his family. He spent decades serving as a cultural and social architect, setting the stage for a flourishing Black Angeleno middle class who owned homes, invested in education, and operated family businesses. His efforts took a huge toll on him in the end.

He would be remembered as a "ready, forceful and a polished writer" by the journalist and archivist Delilah Beasley of The Negro Trail Blazers of California, but his tombstone would read plainly, "Father." Jefferson was a man who fought for all. We find that at the end of his life it seems as if all his freedom fighting reached a final act with the mayoral race of 1913. It was as if all his efforts to establish a model of Black citizenship was leading to this last major battle before his death. It was also at this time that Jefferson began grappling with the state of the Black citizen and what he perceived as their lack of devotion and dedication to collective Black advancement. The pages of *The Liberator* are filled with disappointment and disillusionment as he starts to question the future.

But first, let's explore how he arrived at this point.

Fighting Discrimination

Jefferson spent nearly two decades combating discrimination and segregation in Los Angeles in the town halls and community meetings, and collaborating with churches and voter leagues. A June 14, 1912, article in *The Liberator* challenged the Los Angeles County Board of Supervisors' proposal to segregate the county hospitals and nursing schools and took a stand against segregation in neighborhoods. *The Liberator* encouraged Black Angeleno businesses and homeowners to secure properties in favorable areas around the city. These efforts would come to a screeching halt in the 1920s as restricted conveniences and redlining policies were used more and more to keep some neighborhoods as white only.

These long-standing efforts made by Jefferson and his contemporaries to secure safe, cultured, beautiful environments for Black Angelenos would be an uphill battle. In the essay "The Greatest State for the Negro," Lonnie Bunch describes Jefferson's platform: "Though Edmonds wanted *The Liberator* to be 'read and supported by all classes of people,' he was not afraid to prod, critique, or be controversial. He proudly proclaimed that the paper, 'is a molder of public opinion, not a slave to it'" (Bunch 2001,135). However, by 1913—the last year of the paper—Jefferson was aching for a change. Perhaps he wanted to ensure that his promise of a prosperous, wonderful life in LA was truly possible for newly arrived Black Southerners. Perhaps he already saw on the horizon opportunities closing in on the Black Angeleno community—that all of his work, all of his efforts, might not be enough to create the vision he imagined for the City of Angels.

Shenk Rule: The Final Battle

Jefferson used the pages of *The Liberator* to back John Shenk for re-election as Los Angeles district attorney in the 1911, November election. In the "Good Government Ticket" section of the paper is a single line stating: "Cut this out and take it to the polls with you." According to a December 8, 1911, issue of *The Liberator*, Jefferson encouraged his readers to vote for the re-election of Mayor Alexander "and the entire Good Government ticket to insures the continuation of present prosperity." Shenk was an important figure in the Alexander administration, helping to negotiate the development of the Los Angeles Aqueduct and construction of the Los Angeles Harbor (David 2022). The article continues: "With these gigantic enterprises in operation the value of real estate will be enhanced and the revenue derived from them will reduce taxation" (*The Liberator* December 8, 1911). Jefferson wanted voters to consider their future investments in the City of Angeles. However, he could not have predicted what would come next.

Shenk won the 1911 election and once he was sworn in, the new district attorney began passing discriminatory court rulings that adversely effected Black Angelenos. Perhaps Jefferson felt responsible for helping to elect a candidate who didn't have the Black Angeleno community's best interest in mind. In response to these revelations, Jefferson spent the better half of 1912 and 1913 fighting against the Shenk-endorsed, Jim Crow–style laws creeping their way into Los Angeles. One very powerful example is the Shenk Rule.

In April 1913, Shenk was tasked by the mayor to investigate a discrimination complaint involving a prominent Black Angeleno businessman, Caleb W. Holden. Holden was charged a dollar for a beer when his white colleague was charged only five cents during a meeting in a local saloon. "When asked the reason, [the bartender] said that Holden was charged a dollar because he was a Negro. The matter was immediately referred to the proprietor of the saloon, who stated that the bartender had carried out his orders. The gentleman who invited Holden into the saloon, reported the matter to the Mayor, and asked that the saloon license be revoked on the grounds that he was practicing extortion" (*The Liberator* April 18, 1913).

A *Los Angeles Times* article printed in *The Liberator* two years earlier, April 7, 1911, reported that Holden was denied a land deed for a purchase he made of a vacant lot for $1,000. The seller, Mrs. Scarborough, a white woman, enlisted a real estate agent to sell the vacant lot adjoining her home with strict instructions that it was "not to be sold to a negro." Holden worked with Lewis A. Butland, who purchased the land on his behalf. Once the deed was handed over to Holden, Scarborough refused to accept Holden's payment on the grounds that the funds were acquired by fraud. This discrepancy made its way to the Superior Court, but ultimately the case was dismissed. Holden was a savvy businessman who knew how to work the system.

John Shenk's investigation concluded that the saloon was not at fault and that charging different prices for Black Angelenos was legal for Los Angeles businesses. Jefferson argued in *The Liberator* that "Mr. Shenk completely nullified the Civil Rights bill in this state." Shenk stated that "it was neither extortion nor a violation of the Civil Rights Act to charge a negro more for an article than a white man" (Flamming 1994, 214). It is entirely possible that District Attorney Shenk considered Holden's previous court case and used the saloon discrimination investigation decision as a warning for Black Angelenos. Perhaps he chose to send a message that you can't bypass the systems, and white business owners and lawmakers in Los Angeles would have the upper hand when it came to decision-making.

Nevertheless, *The Liberator* fought back and called out the rising tide of discrimination. "A half block from our office are several coffee houses; we frequently called there at the noon hour for a cup of coffee. The fact that the patrons of these places were sober, orderly business people, there was the most cordial relations between the patrons. As soon as Shenk handed down his infamous ruling, the proprietors of the places demanded fifty cents for a cup of coffee, pointing to Shenk's ruling as authority" (*The Liberator* April 18, 1913).

When Shenk announced his candidacy for the mayoral race of 1913, *The Liberator* printed letters from concerned voters and wrote articles that warned the public of the grave danger of electing Shenk as next mayor of Los Angeles. "Mr. Shenk, as City Attorney, went out of his way to encourage certain business people to violate the law, and a public official guilty of such a violation of his duty is an unsafe man to put at the head of a great, growing, cosmopolitan city like Los Angeles" (*The Liberator* April 18, 1913).

Jefferson used *The Liberator* to encourage Black women voters to stay engaged for this pivotal mayoral race, proclaiming that "colored women must vote early." He asked mothers to reminder their husbands and children to get out and vote. He dedicated pages and pages of the paper to highlighting all the meaningful social organizing and network-ing happening behind the scenes by Black women voter clubs, all in efforts to help keep Shenk out of office. "The ladies of the Rose Cam-paign Committee will hold their final campaign rally at Scott's Hall, 561 Central Ave., June 2nd. As the entire Woman's Rose Campaign Com-mittee of fifty prominent colored women, representing every section of the city, are taking a hand in this great rally, it bids fair to eclipse anything of the kind ever held in the city" (*The Liberator* May 30, 1913).

While Jefferson was encouraging and uplifting the great canvassing work of early Black women voters, he was also using laser-sharp lan-guage to call out by name ministers, journalists, and "poor old professor W. E. Easton" for taking money from the Shenk campaign to sway the Black vote. On the front page of a May 1913 edition of the paper, Jef-ferson printed letters written by Easton threatening Black courthouse employees' jobs if they didn't vote for Shenk.

The Liberator would print weekly articles for nearly a year, casting swift judgment against anyone who supported the Shenk campaign and unabashedly urging Black Angeleno voters to vote as a unit.

> The colored ladies thus far who are supporting Mr. Shenk, despite his ruling against the race are: Mrs. Eva Carter Buckner, Mrs. Morgan Robin-son, Mrs. Hurlbert, Mrs. Slaughter, Mrs. Nellie M. Reed, Mrs. Oliver and Mrs. Malcom II. Patton. Of course these ladies know the widespread, baleful effect the Shenk ruling has upon the rights of the race in this city. And if Mr. Shenk, with their aid, should happen to be elected these same ladies will be called upon to pay a dollar for a five cent dish of ice cream or a cup of coffee at any restaurant whose proprietor should feel disposed to insult them. Well, we judge they will be able to pay the dollar as we are informed that four of them are receiving six dollars per day each for supporting Shenk. If each of the seven receives the same pay they earn together $42 per day. That isn't bad you see, if this money is set aside for dollar ice cream, Mr. Shenk's campaign will furnish them enough ice cream to freeze an elephant stiff. These ladies will be around to see you in a day or two, look them over carefully, give them your sympathy, but give Judge Rose your vote.
>
> (*The Liberator* May 23, 1913)

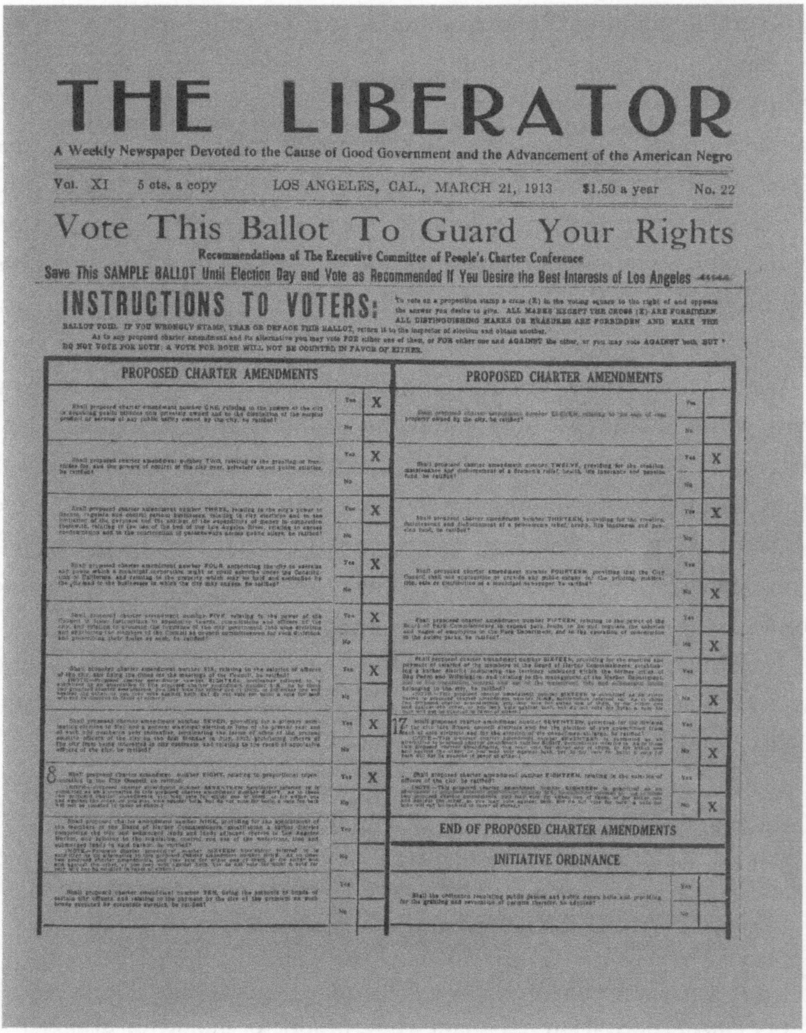

THE LIBERATOR

A Weekly Newspaper Devoted to the Cause of Good Government and the Advancement of the American Negro

Vol. XI 5 cts. a copy LOS ANGELES, CAL., MARCH 21, 1913 $1.50 a year No. 22

Vote This Ballot To Guard Your Rights

Recommendations of The Executive Committee of People's Charter Conference

Save This SAMPLE BALLOT Until Election Day and Vote as Recommended If You Desire the Best Interests of Los Angeles

INSTRUCTIONS TO VOTERS: To vote on a proposition stamp a cross (X) in the voting square to the right of and opposite the answer you desire to give. ALL MARKS EXCEPT THE CROSS (X) ARE FORBIDDEN. ALL DISTINGUISHING MARKS OR ERASURES ARE FORBIDDEN AND MAKE THE BALLOT VOID. IF YOU WRONGLY STAMP, TEAR OR DEFACE THIS BALLOT, return it to the inspector of election and obtain another.

As to any proposed charter amendment and its alternative you may vote FOR either one of them, or FOR either one and AGAINST the other, or you may vote AGAINST both, BUT DO NOT VOTE FOR BOTH. A VOTE FOR BOTH WILL NOT BE COUNTED IN FAVOR OF EITHER.

PROPOSED CHARTER AMENDMENTS

PROPOSED CHARTER AMENDMENTS

END OF PROPOSED CHARTER AMENDMENTS

INITIATIVE ORDINANCE

Figure 8.1 Cover page of *The Liberator*, March 21, 1913. Courtesy of the Edmonds Family Liberator Collection with the Los Angeles Public Library. Digitized by California Revealed.

No Negro paper that has the interest of the race at heart can support Shenk.

If the Negroes want to encourage certain white dealers to insult their women by charging them one dollar for a cup of coffee or a glass of soda, vote for Shenk.

There is but one way—vote against him and see that your neighbor does the same.

Here are a number of Negro traitors sneaking from house to house working for Shenk. Drive them from your door; they would sell your innocent daughter to a libertine for a dollar (*The Liberator* May 2, 1913).

Jefferson was relentless, ruthless—desperate, even. Month after month he reprinted the story leading up to the Shenk ruling to drive home all the discriminatory practices taking place at ice cream parlors, coffee shops, and restaurants in downtown LA. It was as if Jefferson was leaning into his schoolteacher days; the repetition was meant to sink in and help galvanize the Black vote. He printed the ballot on the front page of the April 11, 1913, edition, encouraging voters to bring the paper to the polls as a guide during the voting process. All his efforts in using the Black vote to sway the election resulted in Shenk losing and Henry Howard Rose winning the mayoral race for 1913. Jefferson boasted in the June 1913 edition: "The vote for mayor: Rose, 46,046; Shenk, 38,009. *The Liberator*'s choice is the choice of the people." He went on to share that out of the 15,000 Black voters, nearly 95 percent voted for Rose, helping to swing the election. It was a major milestone in Jefferson's political advocacy career.

Colored Men's NonPartisan League
52 Surry Street
San Francisco, Cal

June 6, 1913

J. L. Edmonds,
210 Thorpe Bldg.,
Los Angeles, Cal.

Dear Sir and Friend:—

Congratulations are in order. We have been watching your fight for some time and are more than glad that you have come out victorious. May you live long to keep up the fight for justice and fair play. We trust that Judge Rose will not forget the service rendered. Judge Rose has now the opportunity of his life, and this organization stands ready to unite with you at any time in a state-wide fight for our rights as citizens. The men who have been unfair to us must be made to see the hand-writing on the wall. The organization asked me to write you this letter expressing their gratitude for the victory you won in your fight for Judge Rose.

I remain,
Sincerely yours,
John A. Wylley.
Member Ex. Committee.
Pasadena, Cal., June 4, 1913.

My Dear Mr. Edmonds:—
Now that the battle is over, the smoke cleared away and the victory is on the side of right and justice, I want to extend my congratulations to you and your paper for supporting a man like Judge H. H. Rose. He formerly lived here and I have known him for many years and always found him just and friendly in his dealings with the colored people.

I am,
Yours sincerely,
Frank M. Prince.
209 E. Second St.
Los Angeles, Cal., June 9, 1913.
Mr. J. L. Edmonds,
210 Thorpe Bldg.,
City.

My Dear Sir:—
I learn with much satisfaction that a number of our thoughtful young colored men are arranging a benefit to raise money to help your valuable paper, and relieve it of indebtedness incurred in making a fight for our rights in the last two campaigns. I have witnessed for a number of years your unselfish fight for the rights and advancement of our people; and although I frequently differed with you, I must with others agree that you have always stuck to principle. I think we owe it to ourselves as men to not only give a benefit to aid The Liberator in its struggles, but should give you one dollar each to purchase a plant for your great paper. What we need in this city is an able fearless paper to keep up the fight as you have done for justice and fair play. I have my dollar ready and will be pleased to hear from 5,000 other men and women who see the necessity of having a fearless, independent newspaper to guard our interests. Trusting that the race may have your unselfish services for years to come, I am,

Yours for a strong, independent, free paper.

Austin Lane.
209 E. Second Street.

Changing Times

While the Black California community celebrated the massive voter turnout and ultimate win for Mayor Rose, *The Liberator*'s victory came with several battle wounds. One more pressing challenge was securing an invested subscriber base to help keep the paper in publication. Brewing on the other end was a more public-facing reputational battle between Jefferson and the Los Angeles mainstream press. Jefferson's relationship with the *Los Angeles Times* grew increasingly contentious over the years.

At first, at the turn of the century, Jefferson was often called upon to serve as a contributing writer reporting on the issues of the Black Angeleno community, and he sent letters to the editor asking for support. He urged the *Los Angeles Times* to take a bigger stance against lynchings and crimes against Black Americans. Jefferson's articles for the *Los Angeles Times* had a diplomatic tone, calling on their humanity and leaning on the better judgment of the editor and writers. In a letter on May 30, 1902, Jefferson penned:

> With the destruction of our constitutional rights in the South complete and trial by jury suspended, we stand in the midst of our dead and dying with bowed heads and broken hearts, overshadowed by our white fellow-citizens in the full enjoyment of peace and prosperity, with none to drop for us a sympathetic tear. In the name of humanity and the rising generation, I hope and pray that the white people of this country will do something—do something right away.

In the early years of the paper, *The Liberator* praised General Otis (the owner of the *Los Angeles Times* at the turn of the twentieth century) for his liberal position on civil rights. After all, Otis had supported Jefferson's early political organizing work while a member of the California Afro-American League (Flamming 2005). In a reprint of an article featured in the June 1904 edition of *The Liberator*, the *Times* advocated for its readers to start "looking at the matter calmly, reasonably and without prejudice—if those of us who have been long prejudiced can view the

matter in so fair a light—it is difficult to perceive that anything unreason-
able has been asked on behalf of the negro." Over time Jefferson began
questioning and calling out the fact that although the *Times* printed articles that advocated for "fair play" for Black Angelenos and their rights,
it was still the only city paper that referred to "the negro as a 'coon' and
to the negro woman as a negress." He went on to say, "We believe that if
the managers of that great paper knew the damage done [to] the colored
fellow citizens by creating prejudice and contempt for them, this cater-
ing to the vicious element of society would be discontinued. The damage
done the negro by this kind of journalism is inestimable" (*The Liberator*
March 1905).

In response, the *Times* attempted to encourage its readership to let
the Black community prove that they were worthy of their newfound
citizenship rights. "The negro asks no more than simple justice. This he is
clearly entitled to, and this he will eventually receive, if he has the patience
to wait for it and the courage to win it" (*Los Angeles Times* reprint in *The
Liberator*, June 1904).

The framing of "earning" or "fighting for your rights" is deeply rooted
in the foundation of the country and echoes in the consciousness of
some of America's first settlers, the Plymouth Rock Pilgrims. Those early
agrarian separatists of the English church, who were deemed heretics and
traders of their home country, fled to The Netherlands to practice their
religion freely; they would later strike up a deal with the Virginia company to become settlers of the "new land" of America (Flynn 1996). The
seeds they carried with them were of war, rebellion, extremism, and the
need to "fight for your rights." They planted those seeds in almost every
facet of the American system; they laid those seeds in the constitution,
the educational system, the penal system, and the high courts of law.

Jefferson was a man who had experienced not one but two major constitutional amendments in his lifetime. He'd experienced state- and citywide policies and laws that granted him and his community civic participation. He was a believer that if the Black community could fight
hard enough, if they could "prove" that they were upstanding and educated citizens, homeowners, and taxpayers, and that if they could come
together to rally against discrimination and bigotry, they could live a life
of peace and enjoy their newly granted civil liberties.

In the end, after all his efforts, we find Jefferson slowly coming to terms with the fact that perhaps the crops that those original pilgrims planted were really only meant for their descendants and not his. This great American harvest that Jefferson worked so hard to cultivate, care for, and nurture was slipping from his fingers, leaving him starved with an ache of displacement and sorrow. He had the courage to leave the South, not unlike refugees who are forced to resettle in new land and rebuild. His children would be first-generation Americans, first in his bloodline to be born with civil rights, so-called freedom. While it's uncommon to use terms like "refugee" and "first-generation" for Black Americans who were forcibly brought to America, the terms still fit. Jefferson believed in the American dream, this great American harvest, because he saw how much civic change unfolded in his own transformational life. However, what we see in the final year of his life is Jefferson coming to terms with the fact that these injustices he'd been battling were in fact deeply systemic.

With this newfound framing, Jefferson grew more and more critical of the skewed, unjust reporting on the Black community within the mainstream press. He was featured less and less as a correspondent as he became more of an agitator, demanding accountability and fairness from the mainstream press. This caused the relationship with the *Times* to turn cold and vicious in the days and months leading up to the October 10 vote for the new mayor. "The fact that the Times and the Express and Tribune have buried their differences and are supporting Shenk for Mayor is proof that some conspiracy is being hatched against the working people, who pay all of the taxes" (*The Liberator*, May 30, 1913). These public callouts led the *Times* to retaliate with a brutal article referring to Jefferson as a "pamphleteer, always looking for a political handout," reporting that he "flung at the [police] department every vicious criticism that he could muster . . . he corrupted many sheets of clean white paper to spread his criticism" (*Los Angeles Times*, October 13, 193).

The sting of those words echoed and rang loudly. Jefferson would go on to print only a few more editions after these *Los Angeles Times* reports.

CHAPTER 9

The Year 1913

The days of Biddy Mason fighting in the courts for her freedom, or Black businessmen and women opening restaurants and hotels and parlors in the bustling downtown LA City center, or Jefferson and his business partner, Noah D. Thompson, purchasing and reselling plots of sprawling farmland to newly arriving Black Angelenos—were coming to an end. Redlining and restrictive covenants, meant to exclude homeowners and business owners from desirable areas based on race and religion, would be in full swing by the 1920s. However, cases of housing discrimination were already taking root in Los Angeles at the turn of the century.

Jefferson had seen this before. He had seen this grand big opening—a promise of a new life, a new type of freedom—only to have it ripped away from him, the promises rerouted, dreams deferred, and yet another roadblock he'd have to bypass.

The following three pivotal points in Jefferson's life are all centered on constitutional changes and statewide mandates meant to protect his rights and help shape a progressive, forward-moving Black citizenship. And yet the laws of the land fell short. Jefferson was forced again and again to rise up and demand that the laws be upheld to the highest standard. I can't imagine the distress and sheer exhaustion he must have battled as he continued to hold tightly to the promise of hope and change.

First, he was told that he and his family would leave the plantation, that the Civil War was over and that Lincoln in Washington had freed them from bondage. He was forced to sign an X for his name and stay as a sharecropper for years before finally attending teaching school in his twenties in northern Mississippi.

Second, after the passing of the 18th Amendment that allowed Black men the ability to vote, Jefferson took to the streets and begin canvassing and registering voters in the state of Mississippi. His efforts were met with violence and death threats. These attacks forced him to start working on the trains and head westbound.

And lastly, third, Jefferson fought for the civic advancement of the Black Angeleno community for so long and hoped to create a California oasis for the Black family, only to witness the city of Los Angeles introducing more and more discriminatory policies. Even when the State of California passed the Dibble Act, a law that mandated that Californians "of every color or race whatsoever" would have equal entry to public places, the discrimination still persisted (National Parks Service 2019). Jim Crow–style laws continued to restrict Black Angelenos from a more liberated life on the West Coast—the antithesis of the promises Jefferson made in *The Liberator* at the turn of the century, nearly a decade prior.

Most readers of *The Liberator* wouldn't know it at the time, but 1913 would be Jefferson's last year as editor of the paper. His daughter Sallie passed away in August of 1912, months into the Shenk versus Rose mayoral race. Sallie was the paper's secretary and worked hand-in-hand with Jefferson: "Sallie was not only the individual favorite of each member of the family but was the universal favorite of her schoolmates. She was full of life, and companionable; always seeing the humorous side of things," Jefferson pined in a brief memorial about her passing in *The Liberator*. The grief, the trauma he endured, the repeating pattern of opportunities opening and closing with such force, all must have chipped away at his spirit. This final battle took the wind out of his sails:

> Friend, the editor of this paper is an ex-slave more than 68 years old who has devoted his time to the work of bettering the moral and intellectual condition of the Negroes continuously since 1873. Fifteen years of which time were spent as a teacher in the public schools of Mississippi. Now, since he is still devoting his entire time to the uplift of the Negro people,

he asks the men and women of the race to devote only $1.50 to the cause by sending a year's cash subscription to *The Liberator*. Send *The Liberator* to your friends in the seat as a New Year's gift; they will appreciate it.

(*The Liberator* January 10, 1913)

Request after request asking for the community to invest back into *The Liberator* didn't yield the returns he had hoped for. At the end of 1913, Jefferson became bedridden. Yet still he is found requesting that "all delinquent subscribers to show their loyalty by promptly sending in a money order for amounts due" (The LIberator September 5, 1913), despite his doctor's orders to take it easy and rest. Maybe after all the fighting, organizing, and rallying, he didn't quite know how to rest.

Jefferson saw his life's work unraveling, changing, shifting. His paper was struggling to keep subscriptions, and he saw the strong community ties he'd help cultivate lose their relevance. A painful bitterness, an exhaustion, and quite possibly a deep-seated sadness began to cast a shadow over his words.

He shared in an article in the April 11, 1913, edition:

On his arrival he rushes to a white newspaper office and advertises his business and this gives his enemies an opportunity to defeat his plans. Nobody does this but Negroes. There is hardly a place in the United States where the intelligent, thrifty Negroes with money, are wanted; and it is high time the Negro knew it. The low, ignorant, vicious, anarchistic foreigner is welcome; but the intelligent, law abiding, thrifty, tax-paying Negro is not wanted. Did you ever hear of a Japanese or a Jew going to a white newspaper to advertise his future plans?

Leading up to the mayoral election, in the middle of 1911, Jefferson had begun criticizing the value and impact of the LA Forum, the same organization he had helped to build and nurture over the years:

It is noted with regret that every one of the many business and professional men of this city have ceased to attend the Forum. The fact that these men are all educated, trained thinkers; makes their absence from the Forum all the more regrettable. If there ever was a time when negro organizations needed the guidance of the educated, trained men of the race, it is now. The absence of these gentlemen from the meetings of the Forum is due to no fault of their own. They formerly attended and lent dignity to its proceedings. It is time for our business and professional men to get together and organize a historical and literary society such as the Bethel of Washington City, and have a place where the people can get the benefit of the trained minds of the race through debates and lectures. The great mass of the colored people of this city are thirsting for knowledge and will fill any hall where there is a chance to obtain it through lectures and discussion of public questions. Life is too short and the need of information too great to waste time listening to people who insist on speaking without thought.

(*The Liberator* May 26, 1911)

On a national level, the year 1913 marked the fiftieth anniversary of the Emancipation Proclamation. Perhaps this fact is what inspired *The Liberator* to engage in a social investigation into the life of the Black Angeleno at the top of the year in 1913. Jefferson visited the home of a prominent Black family in Los Angeles and lamented at the fact that "among the numerous pictures of statesmen and poets that decorated the walls, the portrait of no Negro appears" (The Liberator January 3, 1913). He went on to discover that the home library was void of Black scholars and that the family did not read Black newspapers. A few columns to the right of this article was a brief synopsis of the fiftieth anniversary of the Emancipation Proclamation. Very few Black Angelenos participated in the city wide celebration, and almost no promoted men and women of business were in attendance.

President Woodrow Wilson was signed into office on April 11 and almost immediately began signing off on policies that segregated federal departments and workspaces (Weiss 1969). The same discrimination and segregation efforts happening in Los Angeles were taking place on the national stage. Jefferson, who fought tirelessly for Black citizenship rights and life worth living, was starting to slow down. Perhaps he was coming to terms with the fact that his vision of a just, equitable, and diverse Los Angeles might not come to fruition in his lifetime. He saw his dreams for Black Angelenos slashed when so many of them turned to mainstream media and no longer invested in spirited intellectual debates at the LA Forum. Perhaps his dreams of a Black utopia with the smell of orange blossoms was starting to slip from his fingertips just as his body was starting to give way.

Despite Jefferson's final, more painful sentiments in *The Liberator*, he was still a Black "California booster," dreamer, and visionary; he was still a futurist. It's my belief that he held on to hope—even at the end. The best example is his use of poetry gently placed near his fiery political smackdowns, articles that provide some levity and a window into the dreamer part of his conscience. This same side of him seemed optimistic that the constitutional changes he experienced in his lifetime were in fact true markers of American progress. He wanted those amendments to mean something. He wanted his sense of service, his dedication to the Black community and his citizenship, to have weight. He was cashing in on the promises this nation made, and he was living by the creed of his masthead, "Dedicated to the cause of good government and the advancement of the American Negro."

The poem titled "God's Days and Mine" by Robert J. Burdette, included in the April 11, 1913, edition, must have given Jefferson some relief—some solace that maybe he didn't have to be tied to his past and that he didn't have to hold on so tight to the future. With all his efforts and all his good intentions, he would only be responsible for the present moment that laid before him:

> There are two days in the week about which I never worry—two golden days, kept sacredly free from fear and apprehension.
> One of these days is yesterday . . . And the other day I do not worry over is tomorrow. There is left for myself, then, nothing but today. And any man can fight the battle of today. Any man can carry the burdens of just one day. Any man can resist today's temptations. This is the strength that makes the way of my pilgrimage joyous. I think, and I do, and I journey, but one day at a time.

After battling a long illness, Jefferson Lewis Edmonds passed away on January 4, 1914, bringing to an end both his life and that of *The Liberator*. One of his eulogies was read by former Los Angeles Mayor Meredith P. Snyder, a man who had graced the pages of *The Liberator* quite often and was a mayor who hired Black Angelenos for civic positions and partnered with the Black press to promote change and progress in the City of Angels. Jefferson's passing was honored and respected by Black publishers around the country. The *Western Outlook* shared this tribute:

> The death of J. L. Edmonds, editor of the Los Angeles Liberator, removes from the scene of action one of the most forceful writers of the race on the coast. He was a man who stood up for his convictions, and seemed to fear nothing. He believed in the right and stood up for the same and was a staunch advocate of manhood rights for his race.
>
> (Beasley 1919, 260)

While *The Liberator* did not survive past Jefferson's death, the Los Angeles Forum that he had established continued to function for an additional twenty-eight years, until 1942. It went on to fight several discrimination battles. Most notable was the banning of a screening of *The Birth of a Nation*. Jefferson's legacy of resilience and service to Los Angeles survives to this day, and his influence set the stage for political power for Black Americans in Los Angeles and the State of California. By the 1920s and 1930s, thousands of Black Southerners started moving to Los Angeles seeking work and opportunities (De Graaf et al. 2001). A thriving new Black middle class would start to bloom. Their children would be the ones who helped usher in the Black power movements in California in the 1960s and 1970s. California doesn't always get credit for being at the forefront of social political Black movements, but the Black Panthers and the Black Lives Matter movement were born in California. All were rooted from the same early Black settlers who were fiercely dedicated to politics, civil rights, and citizenship. Jefferson and his contemporaries laid the groundwork for some of the most progressive and effective Black civic leadership in Los Angeles today. Civic leaders like Karen Bass, Holly Mitchell, and the late Tom Bradley were all major players in helping to shape the city we know as Los Angeles.

*

Jefferson probably didn't know it at the time, but he was the farmer: he planted the seeds. He cultivated and prepared the land. He tilled the weeds. He watered the crops and burned the fields when it was time to start anew. His work didn't end with him. The hopelessness he might have wrestled with at the end speaks to his humanity. I found it humbling to see some of the doubt that crept in. It made him real. It made his life mission relatable and accessible.

What a gift it's been to help piece together the records Jefferson left behind. It's been one of the great joys of my life to put all the puzzle pieces in order. I had parts to collect, and so did my dad, my grandpa, and his sister and her kids. We all had a hand in collecting. What an honor to curate all these disparate pieces into a loving collage of memories, historical accounts, painful American policies, poetry, and love.

For the rest of my life, I'll be discovering and rediscovering the lessons of resilience and unconditional love through Jefferson's story. He planted flowers despite all the barriers and all the isolation he felt being a caretaker of such a heavy dream. He tended to his garden and showed others how to harvest and feed themselves along the way. At the same time, he lovingly constructed a blueprint for me, my family, and Black Angelenos then and now.

How could I follow in his footsteps? How could I even get out from behind that shadow? I decided to get very quiet, close my eyes, and ask these questions. What was whispered back to me was . . . *Enjoy your life. Enjoy your family. Enjoy your time together. Remember all of us loved you so much that we laid a foundation for you. We will show you how to do the same. You don't have to worry if it makes sense. It's been done before. You carry with you all of our plans. You aren't starting from scratch. Wait for us in the forest. Wait for us near the trees in your backyard, at the beach. Listen for us when you feel the breeze. We are always with you. Always. Always. Always.*

Epilogue

Note to Adina, Our Queen Califa, and All Those Who Dared to Face the Sea

My Beloved Adina,

I want you to know the mythological roots that keep your maternal ancestors tethered to the land of Angeles and the beautiful state of California.

The story goes that Spanish Conquistador Hernán Cortés, the man responsible for violently ending the Aztec Empire and ultimately annexing mainland Mexico to the Spanish crown, was the same man who gave California her name. It is said that he was reading the 1510 six-part novel series *Las sergas de Esplanadián* (*The Adventures of Esplanadián* by poet Garci Rodríguez de Montalvo) while on one of his many voyages between Mexico and Spain (Hale 1864).

One of the main characters in the series is the notorious Black warrior Queen Califa, who lives and rules over an army of Black Amazon women on the island of California. As Cortés was traveling up to northern Mexico he discovered a peninsula (modern-day Baja California) and found the terrain to be similar to the description of the Island of California in *The Adventures of Esplanadián*. The island was said to be situated on "the right hand of the Indies" in the March 1864 *Atlantic Monthly* article titled "The Queen of California," an essay that includes a transcription of the original series: "Their island was the strongest in all the world, with its steep cliffs and rocky shores" (Hale 1864, 266). Queen Califa was described as one of the most beautiful women of the world with her arms adorned with gold. She and her army of Amazon warriors rode flying griffins and had massive fleets of navy ships in their harbors. The action really begins when she is persuaded to join as an ally to a Muslim king who is battling in a holy war against a Christian nation for control of the city of Constantinople. It's a long, harrowing tale with love, betrayal, adventure and several twists and turns.

The state of California, much like her mythological namesake, Queen Califa, draws visitors from around the globe, commands attention, and exudes an air of mystery and intrigue. Entrepreneurs, business owners, investors, inventors, and artists alike come to California to create a name for themselves. The tech industry was birthed in California, not to mention all the thousands who set out to seek fame and fortune from the Gold Rush at the start of 1848. Today, California produces most of the agricultural products for the country and has the fifth-largest economy in the world. California continues to be at the forefront of civic innovation and environmental justice. All this greatness is wrapped up in the foothills, deserts, and poppy fields spanning our beloved state, and yet still very few know of the fearless Black warrior queen who gave California her dreamy essence and powerful myth.

Many come to California and don't invest in her history or her majesty. Instead, they focus their attention on making use of her natural resources for personal and professional gain. So often they take and don't replenish. Just as Queen Califa was asked to use her fierce warrior prowess in a battle that was not her own, the state of California has been and continues to be treated very similarly—a fate she shares with Black women in America. Black women as a demographic continue to have one of the highest voter turnouts and effectively swing local, statewide, and national elections time and time again. Black women serve as the backbone for countless radical social justice movements in America. Black women have learned to thrive and survive while being fabulous despite all the odds against us. *Baayyybeeee* . . . we will always rise up.

Jefferson knew the value of investing in Black women. He knew that if he poured all his love, devotion, respect, patience, time, and energy into us, the community would thrive. This book is dedicated to all those men and women who were willing to be of service to the advancement of the City of Angels and all her glory, all those who were willing to invest and pour back into our beloved angelic city and help increase her natural riches, all those who planted and tended and harvested new ideals, new ways of thinking, and support for their neighbors.

Jefferson must have learned from the soil that the crops don't need much to thrive—only sun, air, and the right environment. When examining Jefferson's life closely, you find that he applied those same principles to his civic-building work. He taught all of us that when you have community, self-respect, faith, and civic agency, so many wrongs can be made right. Life wouldn't have to consist of proving your existence, fighting for your rights, or drowning in grief. If given the right ingredients and environment, Black Americans could have the space to just be—just like the crops growing, and just as I sat under the tent at those funeral parties in Ghana year after year.

Jefferson spent a lifetime building toward a more equitable, loving city for Black people in the West. As he tended to his garden, he taught me that when we operate from a place of service all is possible. This book is a thank-you for all those who worked to make Los Angeles a home worth celebrating, nurturing, and respecting. It's a thank-you for all those Black families, children, grandmas, aunties, and uncles who risked it all by traveling to unknown lands westward and bravely took on new lives, new ways of being. I'm sure it wasn't easy, but I hope it was worth it in the end. We are forever indebted to you.

However, we can't continue this love letter to Queen Califa, Black women and California without properly acknowledging the amazing mystery behind the origins of LA's founding date. On September 4th, 1781, the Spanish claimed and established settlements of the city we now know as Los Ángeles, (formally named "El Pueblo de Nuestra Seora la Reina de Los Angeles or *The Town of Our Lady the Queen of the Angels*.) Little did the pobladores, the original Los Angeles settlers, know that exactly 200 years later our Virgo goddess, Beyonce would grace us with her existence on September 4, 1981. These fierce Black women, both in mythology and glittering on global stages, have and will continue to inspire for millennia. They both have been working behind the scenes to help usher in the next wave of innovation and progress for our Black people and our beloved California.

A Retrospective

Black Angelenos Making History Then and Now

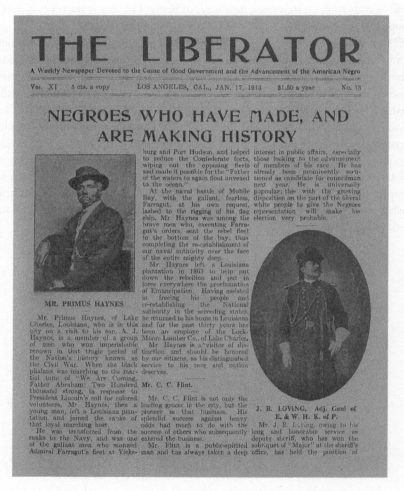

Figure E.1 Negros Making History Special Edition, *The Liberator*, January 17, 1913. Courtesy of the Edmonds Family Liberator Collection with the Los Angeles Public Library. Digitized by California Revealed.

Figure E.2 Profiles of Black Angelenos in *The Liberator*, December 1901. Courtesy of the Edmonds Family Liberator Collection with the Los Angeles Public Library. Digitized by California Revealed.

In true Jeffersonian fashion, I couldn't conclude this book without doing a roll call to uplift and celebrate notable Black Angeleno luminaries both in the land of the living and in spirit form. I've included Los Angeles–based business owners, historians, liberation seekers, and elected officials who truly represent the people—just like Jefferson did in *The Liberator* year after year.

According to census records, Black Americans make up less than 10 percent of the population of the City of Angels. And yet Black Californians hold some of the highest positions of power in local, state, and federal government.

I don't believe that is by accident. The Black families who migrated west were on a mission. At the turn of the twentieth century, Jefferson sent out a call, and thousands answered. Those who came were taught how to wield political power, guard their rights, and prepare to lead. Jefferson and all those early civil rights leaders created an ethic and foundation of civic duty as part of their life mission. The following profiles and bios are the children and grandchildren of Black families who migrated out west looking for a fresh start and a chance to redefine their civic destiny.

* * *

I felt moved to start this list off with our beloved former Mayor Tom Bradley. It's fair to say that Jefferson, his cofounders of the LA Forum, and all the Black Angeleno women and men who fought for civil justice in Los Angeles helped pave the way for the innovative leadership of our late, great Mayor Bradley.

Below is an excerpt from my cousin Donna Brooks. My dad and I are on her father's side of the family tree, while Mayor Tom Bradley, her uncle, was on her mother's side. With all the powerful biographical information about him out in the world, I thought I'd open this section with something personal, tender, and loving about Tom Bradley:

> My uncle was Tom Bradley, and I fondly called him "Uncle Tom" all my life, even as an adult. He was this amazing, handsome, kind "gentle giant" in my eyes. Despite his busy life and career, he always made time for me. Reflecting back, when I was in middle school and high school, he spoke at my schools a few times, and always acknowledged me as his niece. When I got married, he was at my wedding; when I had a daughter, he was there for us. Even though his only biological sister (my mother) was no longer with us, he never deserted me. He was always a phone call away, and made it clear not to hesitate to contact him if I needed him or anything. He was my favorite uncle, however I loved them all. He would bring gifts when he travelled; he would bring gifts at Christmas. He would drive to my home unescorted. I would ask him, "Where is your driver?" He'd smile and say, "I don't need a driver." He attended my daughter's graduations. I never saw or heard him speak a cross word in my life. I could go on and on about him. I am still close with my cousins Lorraine and Phyllis, his daughters. Lorraine keeps me and other cousins in the loop anytime there is an event honoring my "favorite uncle." What a blessing he was in my life.

Thomas Jefferson Bradley, better known as Tom, the second eldest son of parents Lee Thomas and Crenner Bradley, was born December 29, 1917, in Calvert, Texas. His parents were sharecroppers who lived in a small log cabin outside of the town. His grandfather was enslaved. When Bradley turned seven, the family moved to Los Angeles.

Tom's parents would eventually get divorced, and his mother and her five children went on public assistance during the Great Depression. Because Bradley's mother had to work, she didn't get home until late every night. Even though she was exhausted from cooking someone else's meals and completing laundry duties, she always fixed a meal for her family for the next day and asked about their schoolwork.

Tom attended Rosemont Elementary School and Lafayette Junior High School and eventually gained admission to the University of California, Los Angeles, on an athletic scholarship in track. In 1940 Bradley joined the Los Angeles Police Academy, and the following year he married Ethel Arnold, whom he met at New Hope Baptist Church. They later had two daughters, Lorraine and Phyllis. Bradley would later receive a degree from Southwestern University School of Law in 1956. He was voted into Los Angeles City Council in 1963 and was elected mayor for five consecutive terms, from July 1, 1973 to July 1, 1993.

The *Los Angeles Sentinel* shared this of Bradley's legacy on September 28, 2023:

> [Tom Bradley] was one of the best mayors of a major city in the United States in the last hundred years. A man of quiet determination, Bradley spent a lifetime bridging racial barriers and used his skills to bring the City together and forming coalitions. Tom Bradley made history as the first African American mayor of a major US city with a white majority.
>
> While he served as Mayor Los Angeles prospered. He changed the city's downtown skyline. Among his other legacies are the start of the subway and light-rail systems.
>
> Bradley also was a driving force to diversify the city's workforce. He opened doors for minorities and women to not only serve on city commissions, with his leadership black men and women held more management positions. Bradley positioned the City to take its place as an international trade center. He brought the city a glowing spot on the world's center stage with its smooth and lucrative hosting of the Olympic Games in the summer of 1984.
>
> (Cooper 2023)

Bradley passed away on September 29, 1998, at the age of eighty. His commitment to furthering the advancement of Black civic leadership and his community continues to be unmatched.

* * *

Mayor Karen Bass is the 43rd Mayor of Los Angeles and the first woman and second African American to be elected as the city's chief executive. With an agenda focused on bringing urgency, accountability, and a new direction to Los

Angeles, she began her term with a focus on housing people immediately and increasing safety and opportunity in every part of Los Angeles. A daughter of our city, Mayor Bass was raised with her three brothers in the Venice/Fairfax neighborhood and is a proud graduate of Hamilton High School. After serving as a front-line healthcare provider as a nurse and as a physician assistant, Bass founded the Community Coalition to organize the predominantly Black and Latino residents of South LA against substance abuse, poverty, and crime, and to pioneer strategies to address the root causes behind the challenges faced by underserved neighborhoods.

She then went on to represent Los Angeles in the State Assembly and was elected by her peers to serve as speaker, making her the first African American woman to ever lead a state legislative body in the history of the United States. Her time in leadership intersected with the Great Recession, and she was honored with the John F. Kennedy Profile in Courage Award for reaching across party lines and making tough decisions to keep the state from bankruptcy while protecting vital services. While representing Los Angeles and Culver City in Congress, Mayor Bass helped protect small businesses during the pandemic, created policy to drive local jobs from federal infrastructure funding, and led the passage of what the *Los Angeles Times* called "the most significant child welfare policy reform in decades." Bass earned her bachelor's degree in health sciences from CSU Dominguez Hills before graduating from the USC Keck School of Medicine Physician Assistant Program and earning her masters degree in social work from USC. Bass's oldest daughter Emilia planned to follow in her mother's footsteps working for social change. The mayor continues to be inspired by Emilia and her son-in-law Michael's passion for life. She has three other children, Scythia, Omar and Yvette, and two grandchildren, Michael and Henry, who live in the Los Angeles area ("About Mayor Karen Bass" n.d.).

* * *

Senator Steven Bradford brings a lifetime of experience to the California State Senate. In over two decades of public service—first as a Gardena City councilmember, then as a state assemblymember, and now as a state senator—Bradford has proven himself to be an unwavering citizen activist. He views himself as a public servant and not a politician. Public service was instilled in him by his parents, who taught him the value of giving back to the community.

Prior to his service in local and state government, Bradford was a public affairs manager for Southern California Edison, district director for the late Congresswoman Juanita Millender-McDonald, and program director for the LA Conservation Corps, and worked for seven years as a marketing and sales representative for International Business Machines Corporation (IBM).

He made history when he became the first African American elected to the Gardena City Council. Over the twelve years that he served on city council, he helped create robust job and economic growth, and stabilized the city's budget. When he was elected to the council, the City of Gardena was on the brink of bankruptcy and was $27 million in debt. There was no money in the bank and employees had not been given raises in over seven years. By the time he left the council, they had eliminated the debt, allocated $8.5 million in reserve, increased employee salaries without raising taxes or cutting essential services, and secured millions of federal dollars for various improvement projects for North Gardena. He also authored and championed ordinances that established the City's Small Business Task Force and the City's Police Foundation. In addition, as a former solid waste director, he brought those skills to bear, helping negotiate some of the lowest trash rates in the county.

Bradford was elected to the 51st State Assembly District in a Special Election in 2009, re-elected in 2010, and re-elected again in 2012, but the second time around, to the newly created 62nd District. While serving in the Assembly, he rose to prominence by becoming Chair of the Assembly Committee on Utilities and Commerce, which had jurisdiction over electricity, natural gas, telecommunications, private water corporations, and other issues related to commerce.

In his free time, you will often find him on the golf course or attending jazz events. He started a Junior Golf program while on the city council, and his favorite community event is the Gardena Jazz Festival, where he serves as the founder and chair. The festival has been celebrated for sixteen years and is one of the most popular events in the South Bay. Bradford grew up in Gardena, where he resides to this day. He coached football and baseball for sixteen years in Gardena's Parks and Recreation League and attended San Diego State University where he earned a Bachelor of Arts degree in political science at California State University, Dominguez Hills. He currently serves on the board of the Mervyn M. Dymally African American Political and Economic Institute, a nonpartisan public policy think tank ("About Steven" n.d.).

* * *

Supervisor Holly J. Mitchell currently serves on the Los Angeles County Board of Supervisors. As the daughter of parents who were public servants and a third-generation Angeleno, Mitchell leads with a deep understanding of the vital safety net LA County provides to millions of families and is committed to ensuring that all residents can thrive.

Supervisor Mitchell is honored to represent the 2 million residents of Los Angeles County's Second District—including the neighborhood she grew up in—Leimert Park, along with the cities of Carson, Compton, Culver City, El Segundo, Gardena, Hawthorne, Hermosa Beach, Inglewood, Lawndale, Los Angeles (portions), Manhattan Beach, Redondo Beach, and a dozen unincorporated communities.

Since being elected to the Board of Supervisors on November 3, 2020, Supervisor Mitchell has made poverty alleviation a countywide priority and has anchored an equitable recovery plan from the health and economic pandemic caused by COVID-19.

Within her first year as Supervisor, with support of the Board of Supervisors, Mitchell passed a landmark countywide guaranteed universal income program, made LA County the first in the nation to phase out urban oil drilling, and strengthened the County's ability to quickly respond to mental health crises among our unhoused residents.

Before serving on the first all-women-led Board of Supervisors in the history of LA County, Mitchell served for a decade in the California Legislature as a representative for the 54th Assembly District and 30th Senate District, both in Los Angeles County. During her tenure, she helped pass over ninety bills—including the landmark anti-hair-discrimination law, The CROWN Act, making California the first in the nation to pass this law ending hair discrimination.

Supervisor Mitchell became the first African American to serve as Chair of the Senate Budget and Fiscal Review Committee. Under her guidance, the State of California successfully built its financial reserves with the passage of three consecutive state budgets—each totaling over $200 billion.

Early in her career, Supervisor Mitchell had transformative leadership opportunities serving as a CORO Foundation Fellow, a legislative advocate for Californians experiencing poverty at the Western Center on Law and Poverty, and working for pioneering legislative leaders like the Honorable Diane Watson.

Before running for public office, Supervisor Mitchell led Crystal Stairs, California's largest nonprofit dedicated to child and family development, for seven years. As CEO, she fought for low-income families across Los Angeles County to gain access to childcare and poverty prevention resources.

As a member of the Los Angeles County Board of Supervisors, Mitchell also serves on the boards of Los Angeles County Children and Families First (First 5 LA), Los Angeles County Metropolitan Transportation Authority, Los Angeles Memorial Coliseum Commission, LA Care Health Plan, and Los Angeles County Sanitation Districts.

Supervisor Mitchell was awarded an honorary doctoral degree of Humane Letters from Charles Drew University and is a proud UC Riverside Highlander (Los Angeles County Supervisor Mitchell Biography).

* * *

Delilah Leontium Beasley was born on September 9, 1867, in Cincinnati, Ohio, to parents Daniel and Margaret. She attended segregated Cincinnati public schools, and by the age of twelve had begun to write and publish short social notices in the local Black newspapers and some white newspapers, such as the *Cleveland Gazette* and the *Cincinnati Enquirer*. She continued to write and publish during high school, and spent time learning about journalism by working for the *Colored Catholic Tribune*. When her parents unexpectedly passed away in the 1880s, she and her siblings were separated, and Beasley was forced to put her journalistic ambitions aside and seek employment as a maid.

Beasley later studied as a hairdresser, then moved on to train in hydrotherapy, medical gymnastics, massage therapy, and nursing. For several years, she worked in sanitariums and resorts in Chicago, New York, and Michigan, but she never let go of her goal to work as a journalist. Around 1910, Beasley moved to Oakland, California, where she took a job as a nurse. She spent her spare time researching Black history and becoming part of the thriving Black women's club movement.

Beasley enrolled in history courses and began training herself in historical research, visiting private and public libraries, exploring archives, and conducting oral interviews with elderly Black residents about their personal experiences. She spent several years examining California newspapers between the 1840s and 1910s, both Black and white, at UC Berkeley's Bancroft Library. She soon began lecturing on Black history and would eventually publish articles in the *Oakland Tribune* and the *Oakland Sunshine*. After nine years of intensive research on Black history, Beasley published *The Negro Trail Blazers of California*, a study of Black pioneers who had largely been left out of the history books, dating back to early Spanish exploration of the region.

In 1923, the *Oakland Tribune* started a new weekly column, "Activities among Negroes," authored by Delilah L. Beasley, who used her voice to highlight the achievements of African Americans, support Black dignity and rights, raise awareness about the barriers that existed for people of color and women, and encourage interracial activities as a means toward building equality. Over the next two decades, Beasley would also serve as an active member of the NAACP, the Alameda County League of Women Voters, the National Association of Colored Women, the Public Welfare League of Alameda County, the League of Nations Association of the California Federated Women's

Club, the Oakland Council of Church Women, and the Linden Center Young Women's Christian Association, and as President of the Far Western Inter-Racial Committee at the Oakland Museum. Delilah Beasley would continue to write, publish, and participate in civic organizations aimed at advancing the rights of African Americans and women until her death in 1934 (University Library at California State University Northridge 2019).

* * *

Kelli Jackson is the second-generation owner of Hank's Mini Market located in the Hyde Park community of South Los Angeles. Hank's is a family-owned curated market that has been proudly serving the community for twenty-four years.

Kelli's heart for her Hyde Park neighborhood stems from her father Hank's dedication to creating a community-centric business in an often-overlooked area. Her master's degree in public art studies from the University of Southern California further developed her commitment to her community and sparked her passion to use public art to help redefine and reimagine places and spaces. Kelli also has a bachelor's degree in business management and the arts from Dillard University in New Orleans.

In 2018, Kelli helped facilitate a large brick-and-mortar transformation project at Hank's Mini Market. This project reinvigorated the store. Today, Hank's provides access to art, healthy food options, and safe spaces through its shopping experience and community partnerships.

A variety of businesses and organizations collaborate with Kelli to bring art exhibitions, monthly nutrition workshops, food giveaways, and more to Hank's Mini Market customers. Today, Hank's is more than a corner store—it's a gathering place for the community and a bright spot in the neighborhood (National Association for the Advancement of Colored People Kelli Jackson Biography).

* * *

These powerful leaders, community builders, business owners, and historians past and present are true Angelenos' advocates. Their tenacity and resilience and compassion for Black Los Angeles would have landed them on the pages of *The Liberator* at the turn of the twentieth century. It felt fitting to end the book with a nod to these community leaders I admire and respect— just like Jefferson did year in and year out.

Acknowledgments

There were a few people who helped me stay encouraged throughout my research and writing process and to whom I owe so much gratitude, love, and appreciation.

First up is my mom, Pamela Payne, and my daughter's godmother, Lenee Richards. They both stuck by me every step of the way. They lovingly urged me to continue the writing process and stick with it, even when I wasn't always feeling confident or sure about the direction. They both reminded me that I have more than enough support to get this body of work done and done well.

My mom has always been my biggest cheerleader. She always encouraged me to pray about my writing and continue to ask Jefferson for guidance and support. She would work with me for hours, reading and rereading passages with me. She helped me through the long nights and early mornings before the baby would get up and take over my day. Thank you for being my right hand, Mommy, I love you.

My husband JoeJoe, who has been my rock this entire process: thank you for keeping me and the baby fed. Thank you for celebrating with me every step of the way. Thank you for having my back and reminding me that all is possible.

Helen Grossman kept her arms open and always let me bounce ideas around, edited my concepts, and gave me the most thoughtful, beautiful feedback. She promised me in the big conference room at HUB LA that when it was time to write my book she would be there. She didn't disappoint. What a gem. What a true friend. Thank you, Helen baby.

Alisa Howard and Desiree Butler stayed up late nights with me to dream up new worlds and always believed that these stories in the book mattered. Thank you. Thank you for being my sister and my heart.

My Aunt Steph and my Uncle James gave me such meaningful creative advice at the start of this book-making adventure. They instilled in me a desire to read and write and create from my heart. They took me to the theater, the library, countless bookstores, record shops, and museums. Together they helped me construct a rich creative interior world. They fed me artistically for years, and for that I thank them both for helping me get to this point.

Lastly, there is Amanda Charles, the LAPL librarian who found my blog from 2009 and asked to interview me about Jefferson and my research. Her unwavering support, encouragement, and excitement about Jefferson and his story is what inspired me to keep going. Without Amanda, most of this work would still be in the shadows. She was the linchpin. She was the one who helped us open the door to all this possibility. She worked on her time off for years, and our family is forever indebted to her kindness, her scholarship, and persistence. Amanda, thank you for being you. The children's book is on the way—promise!

References

"About Mayor Karen Bass." n.d. mayor.lacity.gov/about-mayor-karen-bass.

"About Steven." n.d. Senator Steven Bradford, California State Senate. sd35.senate.ca.gov /biography. Accessed December 2, 2024.

A Treaty of Peace between the United States and Spain. 1899. Library of Congress. Washington, DC: Washington Government Printing Department. October 1.

Bass, Charlotta, ed. 1960. *Forty Years: Memories from the Pages of a Newspaper.* California Eagle Press.

Beasley, Delilah L. 1919. *The Negro Trail Blazers of California.* Self-published.

Blockson, Charles. 2022. "The History Makers A2002.180." *The History Makers,* interview by Larry Crowe, The History Makers Digital Archive. September 5.

Boutwell, George S. 1876. "Mississippi in 1875. Report of the Select committee to inquire into the Mississippi election of 1875, with the testimony and documentary evidence. . .," n.d. Making of America Books, Digital Collection. University of Michigan. https://name. umdl.umich.edu/AEY0467.0002.001. University of Michigan Library Digital Collections. Accessed October 20, 2024.

Broad Ax. 1900. "Negroes for Bryan and Stevenson. The Negro National Democratic League at Its Recent Sixth Biennial Session in Kansas City, Mo., Issued the Following Address to the Public." July 21.

Bunch, Lonnie G. 2001. "The Greatest State for the Negro: Jefferson L. Edmonds, Black Propagandist of the California Dream." In *Seeking El Dorado: African Americans in California,* edited by Lawrence B. de Graaf, Kevin Mulroy, and Quintard Taylor, 129–148. University of Washington Press.

California Eagle. 1914. "Tributes Paid the Late Editor of the Liberator." February.

California Eagle. 1933. "Editor's Life Colorful." November 24.

California Eagle. 1941. "Life Story of J. L. Edmonds Early California Journalist." December 18.

Carney, Judith Ann, and Richard Nicholas Rosomoff. 2011. *In the Shadow of Slavery: Africa's Botanical Legacy in the Atlantic World.* University of California Press.

Cooper, Earl "Skip," II. 2023. "The Legacy of Tom Bradley, The Mayor of the City of Los Angeles." *Los Angeles Sentinel.* September 28.

Cornish, Samuel, and John B. Russwurm. "To Our Patrons." *Freedom's Journal.* 1827. March 16.

Council, W. H. 1902. "The Uncrowned Queen." *The Liberator.* June.

David, Leon Thomas. 2022. "The History of Los Angeles as Seen from the City Attorney's Office." California Supreme Court Historical Society, January. www.cschs.org/wp -content/uploads/2022/01/Legal-Hist-v.-6-Articles-History-of-Los-Angeles-full-text. pdf.

De Graaf, Lawrence B., Kevin Mulroy, and Quintard Taylor, eds. 2001. *Seeking El Dorado: African Americans in California.* University of Washington Press.

Delilah L. Beasley and the Trail She Blazed. 2019. University Library at California State University Northridge, February 19. https://library.csun.edu/sca/peek-stacks/delilah-beasley.

Dickerson, Dennis C. 1983. *Black Ecumenicism: Efforts to Establish a United Methodist Episcopal Church, 1918–1932.* Cambridge University Press.

Du Bois, W. E. B. 1913. "Colored California." *Crisis Magazine.* California Edition, August.

Edmonds, Arianne 2021. "AB 3121 Reparations Taskforce Hearing Members Witness Statement" State of California Department of Justice. https://oag.ca.gov/system/files/media/task-force-witness-edmondsa-statement-120721.pdf.

Edmonds, Jefferson L. 1898. "Why Are the Colored Voters Supporting the Union Ticket?" *Los Angeles Herald*, October 16.

Edmonds, Jefferson L. 1909. "How Freedom's Word Found the Bondman." *Los Angeles Daily Times*, February 12.

Flamming, Douglas. 1994. "African-Americans and the Politics of Race in Progressive-Era Los Angeles." in *California Progressivism Revisited*, edited by William Deverell and Tom Sitton, 203 –228. University of California Press.

Flamming, Douglas. 2005. *Bound for Freedom: Black Los Angeles in Jim Crow America.* University of California Press.

Flynn, John. 1996. "Africans in America; the Terrible Transformation, (1562–1750); Interview with John Fynn, 1996." WGBH. Video. openvault.wgbh.org/catalog/V_6C7AC02BAE3340C8964610DC11FFB280.

Foner, Jack D. 1974. *Blacks and the Military in American History.* Praeger.

Fuentes, Marisa J., and Deborah G. White. *Scarlet and Black.* Volume 1, *Slavery and Dispossession in Rutgers History.* Rutgers University Press, 2016.

Grimé, William, ed. 1976. *Ethno-Botany of the Black Americans.* Reference Publications.

Hale, Edward Everett. 1864. "The Queen of California." *The Atlantic*, March, pp. 265–278

Howell, Ricardo. 2009. *Mother Bethel AME Church: Congregation and Community.* University of Pennsylvania Press.

James, Winston. 2010. *The Struggles of John Brown Russwurm: The Life and Writings of a Pan-Africanist Pioneer, 1799–1851.* NYU Press.

Jefferson, Alison Rose, Teresa Grimes, Amanda Duane, Jenna Kachour, Allison Lyons, Sean Morales, Emily Rinaldi, and Audrey von Ahrens, for the City of Los Angeles. 2018. "Los Angeles Citywide Historic Context Statement Context: African American History of Los Angeles." *Survey LA: Los Angeles Historic Resources Survey.* planning.lacity.gov/odocument/7db8747f-87fb-4c6f-bb95-5482be050683/SurveyLA_AfricanAmericanHCS_05242019.pdf.

Los Angeles County Supervisor 2nd District Holly Mitchell, 2023, mitchell.lacounty.gov/.

Lembeck, Harry. 2015. *Taking on Theodore Roosevelt: How One Senator Defied the President on Brownsville and Shook American Politics.* Prometheus Books.

The Liberator. 1913. "The Editor on the Sick List." September 5.

Lindahl, Chris. 2019. "Abolitionist Owen Brown's Altadena Grave to Be Preserved in Compromise with La Vina Developer." *Pasadena Star News*, January 14. https://www.pasadenastarnews.com/2019/01/14/abolitionist-owen-browns-altadena-grave-to-be-preserved-in-compromise-with-la-vina-developer/.

Los Angeles Herald. 1908. "Taft Not Popular with Colored Vote." May 31. cdnc.ucr.edu/?a=d&d=LAH19080531.2.46.

Los Angeles Times. 1902. "A Cry from the Black Race." May 30.

Los Angeles Times. 1902. "South Pasadena." May 12.

Los Angeles Times. 1904. "Memorial Service for Ruth Brown Thompson. Large Gathering and Touching Tributes to Memory of John Brown's Daughter—Resolutions to Be Presented the Family by the Forum Club." January 25.

Los Angeles Times. 1907. "Letters to the Times: Let Those People Go." September 13.

Los Angeles Times. 1913. "Why Edmonds Threw Dust" October 13.

Mikell, Robert. 2017. "The History of Allensworth, California (1908–)." Blackpast.org, September 27. www.blackpast.org/african-american-history/history-allensworth-california-1908/.

MLK Community Healthcare. Dream Council. 2024. https://www.mlkch.org/dream-council/kelli-jackson.

National Park Service. 2018. "John Harris Sues Adolph Sutro for Discrimination" April 4. https://www.nps.gov/articles/john-harris-sues-adolph-sutro-discrimination.htm.

Nelson, Stanley, Jr., dir. 1999. *The Black Press: Soldiers without Swords.* Film. Third World Newsreel.

Neuman, Scott. 2021. "A North Carolina City Begins to Reckon with the Massacre in Its White Supremacist Past." NPR. www.npr.org/2021/11/10/1053562371/1898-wilmington-coup-massacre.

New York Age. 1928. "Eloise Bibb Thompson, Playwright, Author Dead after Long Illness." January 14.

Reiniche, Angela. 2023. "Bridget 'Biddy' Mason, the California Trail (U.S. National Park Service)." National Park Service, March 7. www.nps.gov/articles/000/bridget-biddy-mason-the-california-trail.htm.

Richardson, Allissa V. 2016. "The Platform: How Pullman Porters Used Railways to Engage in Networked Journalism." *Journalism Studies* 17, no. 4: 398–414.

Sharpe, Maxine G., Marlissa Briggett, Deborah A. Reid, Peter Reilly, Miguel A. Sapp and Michelle Yu, under the general supervision of General Counsel Stephanie Y. Moore and Deputy General Counsel Edward A. Hailes Jr. 2001. "Racial and Ethnic Tensions in American Communities: Poverty, Inequality, and Discrimination Volume VII: The Mississippi Delta Report." US Commission on Civil Rights, February. www.usccr.gov/files/pubs/msdelta/ch3.htm.

The Liberator. 1901. "Shall Their Home Be Sold?" June.

The Liberator. 1901. "Phenomenal Progress of the Negro Race." September.

The Liberator. 1902. "Mayor Snyder's Great Victory." December.

The Liberator. 1902. "The Republican Policy Outlined by the Call. How the Race Problem Is to Be Settled. Color of the Skin to Be the Test of Citizenship." May.

The Liberator. 1903. "Washington's Great Ovation." January.

The Liberator. 1904. "Mr. C. W. Brooks." January.

The Liberator. 1904. "A Masterly Plea for Fair Play." June.

The Liberator. 1906. "Items of Local Interest." February.

The Liberator. 1905. "The Times and the Colored Folks." March.

The Liberator. 1906. "Dunbar No More." February.

The Liberator. 1906. "Major Allensworth." February.

The Liberator. 1910. "Not Going to Africa." October.

Liberator. 1910. "F. H. Crumbly Real Estate & Notary Public." November.

The Liberator. 1910. "The Truth about Liberia." November.

The Liberator. 1911. "Women Suffrage." March 31.

The Liberator. 1911. "Woman Who Sold Lot Declines to Accept Money from Negro Who Bought Property from Purchaser." April 7.

The Liberator. 1911. "Young Peoples Societies. The Douglass." April 28.

The Liberator. 1911. "A Regrettable Fact." May 26.

The Liberator. 1911. "The Forum." April 28.

The Liberator. 1911. "The Forum." June 16.

The Liberator. 1911. "The Forum." June 23.

The Liberator. 1911. "Miss Marguerite Prince." July 23.

The Liberator. 1911. "Santa Monica." September 1.

The Liberator. 1911. "Quotations from Lincoln, Summer and Other American Statesmen Who Favored Women's Suffrage." October 6.

The Liberator. 1911. "Mayor Alexander Re-Elected Majority 34,000." December 8.

The Liberator. 1912. "California Republicans Closing the Door of Hope." June 14.

The Liberator. 1912. "I Would Like to Correspond with You." April 26.

The Liberator. 1912. "Why Negroes Should Own Farms in California." April 12.

The Liberator. 1912. "We Have Carried California for Wilson." November 15.

The Liberator. 1913. "Seeking Outside Ideals a Foe to Pride of Race." January 3.

The Liberator. 1913. "Negro Families Arrive." April 11.

The Liberator. 1913. "We Need Your Help." January 10.

The Liberator. 1913. "Shenk's Adroit Ruling as City Attorney in Favor of Race Discrimination against the Negro." April 18.

Liberator. 1913. "Twenty Three Hundred Colored People Packed Temple Auditorium to Hear Dr. Du Bois." May 16.

The Liberator. 1913. "Forty Two Dollars per day". May 23.

The Liberator. 1913. "Told Them What to Say." May 30.

The Liberator. 1913. "Would Give the Liberator's Editor the Liberian Mission." April 11.

The Liberator. 1913. "For Sale." September 5.

Troy, Theodore. 1909. "The Forum." *Los Angeles Daily Times.* February 12.

Tye, Larry. 2004. *Rising from the Rails: Pullman Porters and the Making of the Black Middle Class.* Henry Holt.

Walker, Alice. 1982. *The Color Purple.* Harcourt Brace Jovanovich.

Wallace, Kelly. 2018. "Forgotten Los Angeles History: El Aliso, the Big Tree of Los Angeles." LAPL Blog, April 27. www.lapl.org/collections-resources/blogs/lapl/forgotten-los-angeles-history-el-aliso-big-tree-los-angeles.

Washington, Booker T. 1911. "Mound Bayou and Its Builder. Charles Banks." *The Liberator,* April 28.

Weiss, Nancy J. 1969. "The Negro and the New Freedom: Fighting Wilsonian Segregation." *Political Science Quarterly* 84, no. 1: 61–79.

White, Deborah Gray. 2016. *Scarlet and Black: Slavery and Dispossession in Rutgers History.* Rutgers University Press.

Wohlleben, Peter. 2015. *The Hidden Life of Trees.* Greystone Books.

Wormser, Richard, and Bill Jersey, dirs. 2002. *The Rise and Fall of Jim Crow. Jim Crow Stories. The Brownsville Affair.* Film. Public Broadcasting Service.

Index